LAFAYETTE
COMES TO AMERICA

LAFAYETTE
COMES TO AMERICA

By

LOUIS GOTTSCHALK

THE UNIVERSITY OF CHICAGO PRESS
CHICAGO & LONDON

THE UNIVERSITY OF CHICAGO PRESS, CHICAGO & LONDON
The University of Toronto Press, Toronto 5, Canada

TO
FRUMA GOTTSCHALK

PREFACE

THE centennial of Lafayette's death fell in the year 1934. The occasion was celebrated on three continents. Countries as far separated as Poland and Argentina held commemorative exercises. Exhibitions of Lafayette mementos took place in Warsaw, Paris, New York, and Chicago. Books, catalogues, articles, and speeches, in several languages, poured forth by the score. In Washington, on the hundredth anniversary of the general's demise (May 20, 1934), the Congress of the United States, assisted by the president's cabinet, the Supreme Court, and the leading dignitaries of the army, the navy, and the foremost patriotic societies, met in joint session to hear the greetings of France's president and to listen to the president of the United States deliver a memorial address.

Much of what was said on these occasions was sincere, truthful, and scholarly. But it is the fate of every character important enough to be remembered one hundred years after his death that he has become a symbol of something or other, and that those who remember him associate his name with this symbol rather than with the actual historical figure he once was. This is particularly true of Lafayette, who was a twofold emblem even during his lifetime—the embodiment of Franco-American co-operation and the personification of liberalism in an absolutist world.

In fact, Lafayette became somewhat of a symbolical, mythological figure at the very moment that he emerged from relative obscurity into renown. This happened when, in apparent defiance of his king's prohibition, he embarked upon perilous seas to bring aid to the failing American colonies. Search the contemporary records—periodicals, *nouvelles à la main*, the correspondence of celebrities, the dictionaries of the nobility, the war department's service reports—and you will find him mentioned, previous to that event, but rarely, and then only in connection with his wife's family or as a young officer in the king's armies—a distinction likewise due to the influence of his wife's relations. Examine the available contemporary materials for the light they may shed upon his character. Except for a budding spirit of independence that is to be his saving grace at a crucial moment, you will find him quite ordinary, distinguished from his fellows only by less social poise and greater wealth.

But then there enters into his life a fresh interest, the possibility of a grand adventure, the opening of a new avenue to glory. At first this appeals to him only as a means of escape from an existence in which he is beginning to feel frustrated. Yet slowly—but only slowly—he develops an enthusiasm for the cause and becomes a crusader for freedom and the rights of man. The champion of liberty was born out of his interest in America. Contrary to the popular misconception, it was not because he was already a champion of liberty that he espoused the American cause.

The origin of Lafayette's loyalty to America must therefore be sought neither in his philosophy (as yet, he had none but that of his class) nor in his idealism (it was undeveloped until America entered clearly into his consciousness), but in other considerations. The initial motives for his bold departure to the New World were to be found in a growing dissatisfaction with his lot at home, an increasing desire to achieve glory, and a traditional hatred of the English. Upon these feelings more skilful and sophisticated men played, for reasons of their own and without his ever fully discovering their entire rôles or true intentions. Almost, though not quite, without his realizing it, he was deliberately set up as a symbol, as an appealing "front" for a more sinister following, even in this earliest venture of a septuagenarian life.

Once the venture was successful, Lafayette became a popular hero; and since no one knew very much about him, all began to invent, on the basis of what little they did know. A hypothetical analogy which will illustrate this process is not difficult to conceive. Imagine, for example, in the year 1917 a young man still in his teens, son of one of the richest but none too acceptable families of the Middle West. Marry him to the daughter of one of New York's "400." Have him, for a variety of reasons, become dissatisfied with life in the metropolis, and then have the November Revolution break out in Russia at almost the very moment he has reached the decision that he must no longer remain at home. If he were able to induce a Russian representative to promise him a high rank in the Bolshevik army, he would undoubtedly become greatly interested in Bolshevism and go secretly to Russia if he thought appearances required subterfuge, even though he might suspect (what was hardly possible in 1917 but true of Lafayette) that some members of his government were friendly to his scheme. Yet picture, on the one hand, the pained surprise that his conservative friends and relatives might suffer at such behavior, and, on the other, the enthusiastic joy that the supporters of communism in America would derive from it. For his partisans he would suddenly become the man of courage, honor, and ideals, who exchanged all that was good and lovely for the hardships of a revolution because of his principles, though they would really know very little about his principles or whether he had any at all. If (as happened in 1777, but not in our fictitious case of 1917) nearly all the young man's compatriots were then likewise to take up the same cause, he would become a national figure, a token of the nation's nobler nature even before the nation had itself recognized its nobility. Upon returning from his revolutionary activity, whether he liked it or not (though he would like it), he would find it impossible to destroy the symbol and to resume the old life as a dissatisfied son-in-law of an élite family. What he said and wrote would be, probably without his knowing it, in the new rôle rather than in that of the character he had once actually been. The symbol would slowly become the reality.

Such is the thesis regarding Lafayette that is propounded in the pages which follow. Perhaps this little volume will be considered iconoclastic by some, who will condemn its author as a bad patriot. No one likes to have favorite legends destroyed, least of all those that have become part of the national saga.

What may be called the Lafayette myth is one of these. It is
derived largely from an implicit faith in Lafayette's own account of himself. There is not a single case in the following
pages, however, where anything that General Lafayette said has
been repudiated as deliberately intended to deceive. On the
other hand, in every case, Lafayette's own testimony, whenever
possible, has been checked against other contemporary sources.
Where no more reliable evidence was available, the author has
accepted at its face value the testimony of Lafayette; and wherever there existed any discrepancy between Lafayette's *Mémoires* and more nearly contemporary evidence, he has endeavored to explain it as merely a mistaken interpretation due
to the scantiness of the general's knowledge regarding the point
in question.

Most of Lafayette's biographers have been content to follow
uncritically what he said of himself in his several autobi-
ographies. Their story of the eager lad who burned to champion
the cause of an oppressed nation because of ideals of right and
justice which he had imbibed from the eighteenth-century
philosophers, and who defied his entire government in order to
run to that nation's aid, is here rejected. To those who may
consider this deplorable, it must be said that in the long run
the reputation of Lafayette benefits by the destruction of the
"boy-wonder" legend. He ceases to be a kind of Sir Galahad
whose strength was as the strength of ten because his head was
thick. He becomes instead a young man struggling toward liberal ideas. "It is an extraordinary phenomenon," said Mme de
Staël, "that a character like M. de Lafayette should have developed among the highest ranks of the French nobility."[1] She
should have added that the development was a gradual one.
The champion of lost causes was made only slowly; he was not
born.

In another place[2] the author has said that Lafayette was like
the much decorated war veteran who, when asked by a kindly
old lady how he had earned so many medals, pointed to the

---

[1] *Considérations sur la Révolution française*, I, 143.
[2] "Lafayette," *Journal of modern history*, II (1930), 287.

largest of them and said that he had been awarded that one by error and had received all the others because he had the first. The analogy is, however, not perfect, since, though misrepresented by his biographers, Lafayette's first triumph was entitled to much of the credit that has been given it and many of his later successes were even more deserving. The analogy nevertheless holds true to this extent—that if he had not received exaggerated fame for his first achievement, he might never have risen above the level of his class, might never have received another "medal." If it be iconoclasm to rearrange Lafayette's medals, to insist that the first one be comparatively small and that some of the larger ones come afterward, then the author, though with the greatest reluctance, must admit the fault.

An enumeration of the many institutions and individuals that have aided the author in the preparation of this volume would be long and tiresome, even though his gratitude (in this case certainly a lively sense of favors yet to come as well as already received) is lasting and sincere. Some of those who have put their manuscripts and libraries at his disposal are mentioned in the footnotes and bibliographies. But to all those who have assisted him with materials, ideas, and good will, in Europe and America, whether or not mentioned in this volume, the author wishes to express his thanks and appreciation. To the John Simon Guggenheim Memorial Foundation, the General Education Board, and the Social Science Research Fund of the University of Chicago, which made it possible for him to finance these researches, the author's gratitude is particularly due. And it would be utter thanklessness to fail to acknowledge his indebtedness to his friends, Marshall M. Knappen, who twice read the manuscript in its rough drafts and induced the author to make several emendatory changes, and Hill Shine, who read and corrected the proofs.

Louis Gottschalk

Chicago, Illinois

TABLE OF CONTENTS

CHAPTER I

The Little Lord of Chavaniac

A CONFIRMED tourist would call Chavaniac "pictur-
esque." High among the hills of the upper Loire region,
its fifty or sixty houses huddle close upon each other,
leaving scarcely enough space for the half-dozen roads that
form the village boulevards. Dogs, cows, sheep, goats, pigs,
and an occasional horse share the streets and the buildings with
the few hundred inhabitants. The nearest railway station is
two miles away. But Chavaniac is nevertheless a metropolis for
the still smaller hamlets of the canton, some of them not even
directly connected with a highway. Seen from the heights above
it, the bright-red tiles of its roofs thrown against the white and
gray of its stone walls, framed in the acres of green and yellow
fields round about, Chavaniac looks fresh, clean, and whole-
some. Distance hides the dirt and the smell and the tired faces
of the villagers.

It has changed very little in the last two centuries. There are
now perhaps twenty additional houses, a hundred more inhabitants, and a few automobiles; the roads are a little better, and
the smoke of a railway locomotive can be seen in the distance
from the hills; a cheap monument or two has been placed on
"the square," a modern school building has been erected, and
a few new shops have been opened; the creation of a sanitarium
close by has brought visitors and a kind of prosperity to the
village. But if some eighteenth-century traveler were to return
to it now, he would still find cow-teams pulling the carts, peasant women making lace in front of the houses, and the familiar
marks of live stock upon the streets. Many a resident of the

village has not traveled as far from home as the town of Le Puy, about twenty-five miles distant.

Except in a primitive, rustic fashion, life could not have been very gay here in 1757. Not even the birth of an heir (September 6) to the seignior of Chavaniac disturbed for long the even monotony of the village routine. Circumstances did not permit too great an exhibition of joy. His father was, at the moment, away at the war, and no one knew when he would return. No word had been received from him in several days, and the women of the house were worried and impatient.[1] The child's grandfather, the wealthy Marquis de La Rivière, was to be his godfather, but the long and uncomfortable journey from Paris in heavy coaches over unpaved roads kept him away from Chavaniac. Nobody remembered even to note the room in which the new heir was born, and years later his own son did not know which of the several dozen in the house was his father's birth-chamber.[2]

The baptism the very next day was a somewhat gala affair, however. It was celebrated in the little parish church, which today, restored and redecorated, still occupies its ancient site close to the remodeled château. The absence of the mother, father, and godfather was offset by the presence of the child's cousin, the Abbé de Murat, who was grand vicar of Sens and almoner of Mme the Dauphiness. The abbé held him at the baptismal font. Ever after the boy called him "uncle." His grandmother, Marie-Catherine de Chavaniac, was his godmother.[3] The plain rectangular walls of the simple church had seldom before seen such an illustrious gathering. Many years later, the boy, grown into a somewhat skeptical old man, was able to joke about the numerous saints after whom he was

---

[1] Catherine de Chavaniac-Lafayette to M. de La Colombe, September 6, 1757, Ulysse Rouchon, *Un ami de La Fayette, Le Chevalier de La Colombe* (Paris, 1924), p. 8. For the spelling of Lafayette's name, see Appen. I below.

[2] Jules Cloquet, *Recollections of the private life of General Lafayette* (London, 1835), p. 246. A more recent "tradition" says the birth-chamber was on the lowest floor of the southwest tower; cf. Lida Rose McCabe, "Lafayette's château," *Century magazine*, LXXXIII (1911), 54.

[3] There are several copies of the baptismal record extant. See especially Archives du Ministère de la Guerre (hereafter referred to as A.M.G.), Lafayette, dossier 1261.

named. "I was baptized like a Spaniard," he said. "It is not my fault, and with no intention to deny myself the protection of Marie, Paul, Joseph, Roch, and Yves, I have most often called upon St. Gilbert."[4] But for the little one-day-old Gilbert, the ceremony was a solemn affair. He was being baptized into that church which he was never really to renounce, no matter how far from it he was to stray or how seriously he was to challenge its teachings. Symbols were to play a very serious part in Gilbert's future life; this was only the first of them.

Thus ycleped after numerous holy dignitaries, the boy began a career curiously dominated by women. He never had any recollections of his father. When he grew up, he was not even sure whether he had been born before or after his father's death.[5] He was, however, almost two years old when the Battle of Minden brought this first great tragedy into his life, and made him the Marquis de Lafayette. His father, Michel-Louis-Christophe-Roch-Gilbert du Motier, Marquis de Lafayette, colonel of the French Grenadiers, had gone off to fight the Prussians in the Seven Years' War. At Minden his corps commander, though ordered to keep his men below the horizon, out of sheer bravado exposed them on the crest of a ravine. Lafayette's immediate superior was killed, and when Lafayette, already suffering from shell concussion, stepped up to take his place, a cannon ball fired by an English artillery unit cut him in two.[6]

Colonel Lafayette's only son, barely two years old, now became Seignior Marie-Joseph-Paul-Yves-Roch-Gilbert du Motier, Marquis de Lafayette, Baron de Vissac, lord of St. Romain, Fix, and other places. He was also lord of Chavaniac, but as that was still subinfeudated—held in undertenancy to another local lord rather than directly from the royal family—it was not yet

[4] Lafayette to Mme de Pougens, 11 Pluviose [year not given], Henry Mosnier, *Le château de Lafayette-Chavaniac* (Le Puy, 1883), facsimile at end.

[5] Cf., e.g., *Mémoires, correspondance, et manuscrits du Général Lafayette*, I (Paris, 1837), 6, where confusion as to the date of Minden is obvious.

[6] *Mémoires de M. le Prince de Montbarey*, I, 175–77. M. Emmanual Fabius of Paris owned a letter written by this Lafayette to his wife a few days before the battle, July 28, 1759; see André Girodie, *Exposition du centenaire de La Fayette (1759–1834)* (Blérancourt, 1934), p. 10, no. 5.

mentioned in his title. His father had died without leaving a will, and the widow reclaimed much of his property. The new marquis' grandmother felt obliged to appeal to the king for an allowance to bring him up properly, and the king generously awarded the new-made orphan a pension of 600 livres, or, roughly, about $720.[7] Nevertheless, he was not really poor, for when his mother and grandmother died, he could expect to enjoy an income of 25,000 livres (about $30,000) a year. That would make him moderately rich as country gentry went. Besides, when he was barely four years old, the death of his maternal uncle made him the heir also to the vast La Rivière fortune,[8] and gave him the prospect of an income of 120,000 livres (approximately $144,000) a year. That was a fortune that few even among the court nobility would ever be able to enjoy.

The new marquis was placed under the care of several guardians. His great-grandfather the Comte de La Rivière, his grandfather the Marquis de La Rivière, his "uncle" the Abbé Murat, and another "uncle" Nicolas de Bouillé, Bishop of Autun, his nearest male relatives, became his *tuteurs*, and the lawyer, Jean Gerard, became his legal and financial adviser. Because there were so many in this board of guardians, they all soon adopted an impersonal attitude toward their ward. They seldom, if ever, came to Chavaniac, and so the child was intrusted to his women folk to be brought up. His mother left most of that task to his father's family, for she had a father and a grandfather of her own in Paris, and found it desirable to spend most of her widowhood in the capital. Until he was eleven years of age the boy saw her only a few months a year. He was given mostly to the care of his grandmother and his two aunts.

They were fine ladies, these three. His grandmother was a

---

[7] Marquise de Lafayette to Louis XV, October 6, 1759, E. Charavay, *Le Général La Fayette 1757–1834* (Paris, 1898), pp. 554–55; A.M.G., Lafayette, dossier 1261; and Morizot to Mlle du Motier, October 4, 1779, University of Chicago, DC 146, f. L2A3, Vol. I. Charavay, p. 2, says 780 livres, but this was what the pension amounted to in 1785 when Lafayette surrendered it, the increase being due to accumulated interest. Charavay, following Doniol, refers to Catherine de Chavaniac-Lafayette as Comtesse de Lafayette, but I have seen contemporary records that describe her as marquise; see below, p. 153. For the translation of livres into dollars, see below, n. 18.

[8] Charavay, p. 553.

widow. It was she who had brought the Château Chavaniac into the Lafayette family. She had lived in it since 1701, when it was rebuilt after partial destruction by fire, and was to die there in 1773.[9] She was the pride of the villages round about, renowned for her kindness and wisdom, and the little boy used to admire the gentle way in which she guided the villagers who came to her, sometimes a distance of twenty leagues, for advice.[10] She did more than advise others, however. Her beloved Chavaniac, upon the death of her son, was in part still a fief, and its owner owed faith and homage to its overlord, the Comte de Maillebois. Shortly after her son's death, when her grandson was not yet five years of age (April 7, 1762), she bought the extinction of Chavaniac's feudality. She also purchased other rights in the neighboring territories including the privilege of interpreting the law (*droit de justice*) to the peasantry in the parish of Aurac and other villages near by. Her grandson, on coming of age, was to be no ordinary country squire; he was to owe allegiance to no one but the royal family.

Grandmother Lafayette had two daughters living with her at Chavaniac. The older was Marguerite-Madeleine du Motier. She had never wished to marry because she could not make up her mind to leave the family, and she now devoted all of her affection and "extraordinary merit" to the early education of her orphaned nephew. His other aunt was Louise-Charlotte de Chavaniac, widow of a gentleman who, despite the identity of names, was not one of the Chavaniacs of Auvergne. She had come to live with them when Gilbert was four years old. Young Lafayette soon came to feel that he belonged to her rather than to any of the others, for her little daughter, one year older than himself, became his only friend and playmate.

The two little aristocrats lived in the huge château alone among the older women. The town children were too far away and also too deferential to play with them. They took off their

[9] Gerard to Mlle du Motier, February 23, 1774, in University of Chicago, DC146, f. L2A3, Vol. I.

[10] For this and other details of the family tradition which follow, see "Fragment d'autobiographie" in *La Haute Loire*, September 6, 1883; this is quoted as "Autobiographie de Lafayette par lui-même" in Charavay, pp. 531–36.

hats as the young seignior passed by. Gilbert and his cousin became devoted friends and confidants. "Never did sister and brother love each other more tenderly."[11] In this houseful of widows, old maids, and orphans, three generations of women watched over the little marquis and guided his childish steps.

Life at Chavaniac was not very eventful. The château, perched on a hill, its round towers commanding a view of the mountains studded with tiny red-roofed villages, resounded only to the talk of women folk and the prattle of the two children. When Gilbert was five years old they gave him a tutor, whom he afterward remembered only as an abbé of much intelligence. At seven he received another tutor. This was the Abbé Fayon,[12] to whom he became deeply attached and who remained with him after he had reached maturity.

The Abbé Fayon, a provincial cleric selected by an orthodox grandmother, instructed his charge in the approved fashion. The young lord's formal education consisted of learning how to read and write somewhat better than most boys of his age, but very little more. Much of his spare time was spent in listening to the recital of his ancestors' glories. The family tradition, tenderly taught him by the devout ladies at the château, came to him filled with glamorous details and pious errors. Some of them he believed until the day he died. But the time was to come when, as advancing age brought disillusionment, he was to feel a tolerant contempt for long genealogies and to express approval that his family archives had been destroyed in the French Revolution. Even as he did so, however, he was not able to refrain from pointing out that his ancestors' records were nearly as old as the record-keeping custom itself.[13]

But the more ancient of the family rolls that excited the child's pride were not those of the Lafayettes. For the direct ancestors of little Gilbert, who was one day to make the name of Lafayette renowned in distant lands of which many of his most illustrious forbears had never even dreamed, had come

[11] *Ibid.*, p. 533.

[12] *Ibid.*, and *Mémoires du Général Lafayette*, I, 89 and n. 2.

[13] "Autobiographie," Charavay, p. 531.

by that name only very recently and only by a fortunate series of adoptions and inheritances. The young marquis learned that the family from which he was descended had been a long line of younger sons, in a country where it was the rule that the oldest son should inherit the family title and fortune.

Gilbert's own great-grandfather, for example, has been named, not Lafayette, but Charles Motier de Champetière. Though the Lafayettes, the oldest branch of their line, had flourished about the year 1000, the Champetières went no farther back than the thirteenth century. A glorious poverty soon overtook this younger branch, for it was a family weakness that the men should fall fighting for their kings and that its women should take the veil.[14] Near the close of the sixteenth century the Champetière family also broke into two branches, and when little Gilbert's great-grandfather was born (*ca.* 1650), he was heir only to the cadet branch of the Champetières, who were themselves a cadet branch of the Lafayettes. It was not a very good beginning for a great name and a great fortune.

But Gilbert's great-grandfather, Charles, survivor of many campaigns, retired from warfare to husband his resources. He owned the fine château of Vissac the ruins of which can still be seen a little past the station of La Chaud, on the left of the rail-road track which runs from Le Puy to Brioude. Gilbert had seen it and was erroneously told that the Marshal de Lafayette had built it about 1400. The Champetières were only petty country squires, lost among many others of the same stripe in the mountains of Auvergne. But Charles aspired to something higher, and fortune at first seemed kind. The elder branch of the Champetières was short-lived, and on the death of his cousin the Champetière fortune was once more united in Charles's hands.

Charles also acquired a more illustrious title. The contemporary Seignior of Lafayette had an only child, a daughter, and a younger brother who had become a monk. It looked as though upon her marriage and the death of her uncle the name of Lafayette would disappear forever. In the emergency the Seign-

[14] Bibliothèque Nationale, Manuscrits français 20250, fols. 59-61.

LAFAYETTE'S OUTSTANDING ANCESTORS*

Pons Motier de Lafayette (*ca.* 1000)

Pons Motier, Seigneur de Champetière

Gilbert Motier, Seigneur de Lafayette (*ca.* 1284)

Gilbert Motier (1372?–1464), Marshal of France

Charles Motier
Seigneur de Champetière (*ca.* 1600)

Jean Motier de Champetière
Baron de Vissac

Jean-Gabriel Motier
Seigneur de Champetière (*ca.* 1650)

Charles Motier de Champetière, Baron
de Vissac, who inherited the name of
Lafayette by a will made in 1692

René-Armand, Comte (or Marquis) de Lafayette
(1659–94), son of Mme de Lafayette, author
of *La Princesse de Clèves*, etc.

Edouard Motier de Lafayette (d. 1740)

Marie-Madeleine Motier de Lafayette (married
the Duc de La Trémoïlle in 1706; with
her the older line died out)

Michel-Louis-Christophe-Roch-Gilbert du Motier,
Marquis de Lafayette (1732–59)

Jacques-Roch Motier de Lafayette (1711–34)

Marie-Joseph-Paul-Yves-Roch-Gilbert du Motier (1757–1834), Marquis de Lafayette

* Broken lines indicate omission of several intervening generations.

ior of Lafayette determined that his cousin, Charles Motier de Champetière, should succeed to the name of Lafayette, though the estate was to stay in his daughter's hands until her death. Family tradition had it that the Seignior of Lafayette's will further provided that his little child was to marry Charles and thus preserve the Lafayette lands as well as the name within the family. But the young Mlle de Lafayette finally espoused not her poor country cousin but a rich court gentleman instead. So Charles inherited only a name, empty as yet though promising.

Charles's son, Edouard, was little Gilbert's grandfather. Though he had been quite a soldier in his day, he was of interest to Gilbert only because he had been the husband of his beloved grandmother. Yet it was Edouard who first abandoned the old name of Champetière and called himself Marquis de Lafayette. By his marriage to Gilbert's grandmother he had also increased the family holdings and acquired a finer chateâu. For when Edouard's father-in-law died, Chavaniac was added to the Lafayette possessions. Upon Edouard's death (1740) his children deserted Vissac and went with their mother to live at the newer château. Edouard had felt called upon to play a part worthy of his new name and income. He left the provincial hills of Auvergne and went to the royal court to play his part in society. He became a subaltern in Louis XV's bodyguard. His chief claim to glory, in fact, was that, upon his first public appearance in that capacity, he had the great honor of breaking his head in the royal presence by falling off his horse.[15] Gilbert never heard of that, however, though his grandfather, a hard-headed gentleman, survived several years longer to tell the tale.

It was the next generation that interested young Gilbert the most. Edouard de Lafayette's oldest son was Gilbert's uncle Jacques-Roch. Before this uncle's sixth birthday, his rich Paris cousin, the former Mlle de Lafayette, in accordance with her father's will, left him the seigniory in Basse-Auvergne that was

[15] *Mémoires du Duc de Luynes sur la cour de Louis XV (1735-1758)*, ed. L. Dussieux and E. Soulié (Paris, 1860-65), I, 102; II, 36.

known as La Fayette. Jacques-Roch thus became the first of the Champetières actually to own the estate of the Lafayettes. A charming person, genial of manner, handsome, and brave, at eighteen he was captain of dragoons. His courage cost him his life. In the War of the Polish Election, which France unsuccessfully fought against Austria and Russia in order to place Louis XV's father-in-law upon the Polish throne, Gilbert's uncle served with the army in Italy. One day he led his company in a charge against the Austrian line, drove the enemy back, and captured their commander. Fearing that his men might harm his prisoner, Jacques-Roch placed him on his own saddle behind him. But they soon ran into another Austrian contingent, and the Austrian officer, who had not been asked to surrender his pistol, shot his generous captor in the back.

Jacques-Roch's claims to the Lafayette titles and possessions thus passed to Gilbert's father, Michel-Louis-Christophe-Roch-Gilbert, who was then only two years old. Edouard de Lafayette was still alive, but six years later, when he likewise died, Gilbert's father became the first of the new branch of the family to unite both the Lafayette name, which he had inherited from Edouard, and lands, which he had inherited from Jacques-Roch. When the time came, Roch-Gilbert was able to make his appearance at court and, through a kinsman's influence with the king, secure the royal permission to marry Mlle de La Rivière.[16]

It was a magnificent match. Marie-Louise-Julie de La Rivière was the scion of a long line of Breton nobles, who could trace their descent from St. Louis, king of France. Her father was the Marquis de La Rivière, young Gilbert's godfather. Her mother had been considered one of the most beautiful women of her day and was to become lady-in-waiting to one of the king's daughters. Julie had inherited some of her mother's beauty and some of her father's intelligence.[17] But it seemed highly improbable that she would ever secure much of his fortune. For

[16] *Ibid.*, XIII, 227; XVI, 258.

[17] Cf. portrait of Julie de La Rivière-Lafayette in Allan Forbes and Paul F. Cadman, *France and New England*, I (Boston, 1925), 61; and "Autobiographie," Charavay, p. 533.

when Julie de La Rivière married the Marquis de Lafayette, one of her brothers was still alive, and the bulk of the La Rivière fortune had to be saved for him. A small dowry, nevertheless, was found for her. It was fixed at a sum of money that brought an annual income of 1,000 livres, or approximately $200—perhaps $1,200 in gold today. It hardly sufficed to pay the expenses of the four campaigns the young marquis was soon called upon to fight in the course of the Seven Years' War.[18] But the influence of the La Rivières had brought the young marquis a colonelcy in the French Grenadiers.[19] Since that was a higher rank than any of his branch of the Lafayettes had ever attained, his wedding (May 22, 1754) was a great event in the family annals. The marriage did not last long, however. Five years later the Battle of Minden made Julie de La Rivière-Lafayette a widow and little Gilbert an orphan.

On this story of his family's greatness, decorated with romantic inventions and fictitious details, the receptive mind of Abbé Fayon's little pupil was nourished. The Marshal de Lafayette, who had fought alongside of Joan of Arc against the English, the charming lady who had won the heart but resisted the attentions of Louis XIII by retiring to a convent, the Mme de Lafayette who had been one of the outstanding literary adornments of the preceding reign, were the most famous of his family, but they belonged to the more ancient line and he preferred his own immediate ancestors. The stories of how his uncle's generosity to an Austrian prisoner had cost him his life, and of how his adored father had been needlessly sacrificed to an English cannon, interested him the most. They said that an

---

[18] Marquise de Lafayette to Louis XV, October 6, 1759, in Charavay, pp. 554–55. An eighteenth-century livre was approximately one-fifth of a contemporary American gold dollar. It is very difficult to determine how much more a gold dollar would have bought then than today. Various authorities have estimated it at anywhere from three to ten times as much as in recent years. To arrive at a rough estimate of the current American values of the figures here given in livres, it is approximately correct, though an oversimplification, to divide the number of livres by 5, in order to get the equivalent in eighteenth-century gold dollars, and then to multiply by 10, in order to get some idea of the relative purchasing-power of those dollars as compared with those of 1965.

[19] *Journal et mémoires du Marquis d'Argenson*, ed. E. J. B. Rathery, VIII (Paris, 1866), 275–76.

English officer named Phillips had commanded the battery which mowed down his father's regiment at Minden.[20] He remembered that name; he was to meet Phillips one day and even the score. To hate the English became a filial as well as a patriotic duty.

Being the man of the house had its obligations too—especially in the year 1765. Lafayette was eight years old, when the whole of Auvergne became panic-stricken over a plague, sent by the Lord, as the more devout declared, to punish the irreligious. It was a fearsome beast that came out of the neighboring Gévaudan forest, killed the cattle, and even, so they said, ran off with little children. It was a huge, savage, and terrible animal, everyone reported. It became known as the hyena of the Gévaudan, and famous hunters came to bag it. The king even sent some of his most experienced gamekeepers after it, but it eluded all its pursuers and kept up its deadly forays. Little Gilbert yearned to meet it in his lonely walks among the hills of Chavaniac. With his bare hands he would attack the beast and then face the world as a worthy descendant of his fathers.

But this earliest dream of glory was shattered when the proud lad learned that a certain newspaper, in reporting an encounter between a man and the beast, in which the man's fear had prevented him from killing the animal, gave the name of Lafayette to the frightened hunter. That was too much. The indignant boy sat down and addressed to the guilty journal a vicious letter that a wiser aunt did not send off. The beast of the Gévaudan forest was allowed to continue his career undisturbed by Lafayette for many years thereafter, until in 1787 an animal believed to be the "hyena" was killed, and found to be only a large-sized lynx.[21]

And so, amid his daydreams and the memories of his ancestors, with only women as companions, the boy grew to be eleven. Then came a momentous decision. He must go to

[20] See "Autobiographie," Charavay, pp. 532–33, and also letter of Lafayette to Major-General Greene, Baltimore, April 17, 1781, in the collection of the late Mr. William L. Clements, Bay City, Mich.

[21] See "Autobiographie," Charavay, p. 534, and "Bête du Gévaudan" in Le grand Larousse, II, 645.

school and be brought up like a gentleman. The death of his mother's brother in 1761 had left him the only heir to his rich grandfather. Shortly thereafter his mother had been presented at court.[22] There was now no reason why he should remain a simple country gentleman for the rest of his life. It was agreed that his mother take him away from Chavaniac and make a courtier of him.

In 1768 Gilbert went off to Paris to live. France was for the moment at peace with her neighbors. Louis XV was still king, and Mme du Barry was soon to rule his heart. One group of nobles who rallied behind the Parlements, the country's leading law courts, intrigued against another group of nobles who rallied behind the king and his favorites. It was an atmosphere for which the young and unsuspecting country squire was scarcely prepared.

It hurt the child to leave his beloved Chavaniac, his grandmother, his aunts, and, most of all, his little cousin, and go off with his handsome mother, who was somewhat of a stranger to him, to live in a far-away city. When his carriage left behind the familiar confines of the rocky hills, he noticed that the people they met no longer respectfully lifted their hats to him as he passed. He felt very sad indeed. He was a very little lad, sandy-haired and bright-eyed. His mother and he had sat for a portrait when he was about seven years of age, and the artist had painted him holding a picture of his little cousin.[23] Odd that he should now have only that picture to remind him of his playmate and his beloved Chavaniac. He had no curiosity to see the famous capital. The new life he was about to enter meant nothing to him. He wished he could remain "the little lord of the village."[24]

Gilbert's premonitions were to prove only too sound. He was

[22] Chérin to the Duc de La Vrillière, Paris, March 12, 1774, Charavay, p. 556 n.

[23] The portrait is reproduced in Forbes and Cadman, *France and New England*, I, 61. See also p. 57, and *Mid-week pictorial*, XXXIX (1934), 12, for a reproduction which probably represents the portrait of Lafayette which Cloquet says (p. 264) was painted when he was nine or ten years of age. It is probably this one which Gilbert's mother sent to his grandmother at Chavaniac; cf. Girodie, p. 12, no. 8.

[24] "Autobiographie," Charavay, p. 534.

going from the place where he was master into a world where people would patronize him. Their families were old compared to his. His grandfather and his father had been the only ones of his branch of the family to bear the title of "marquis" before him. The very house in which he lived had not belonged to his father's father. His father's grandfather had not been a Lafayette. Only three generations past, his ancestors had been but a cadet branch of a cadet branch of the Motiers. In fact the "society register" of the day did not even mention him, his father, his grandfather, or any of the Champetière branch of the Lafayettes.[25] And he was the first of his line to have any royal blood in his veins or prospects of real wealth. Both of these came from his mother's side of the family. His father's ancestors had been mere *hobereaux*, simple country squires, whom fortune and wise marriages had at last begun to favor. Where he was now going, people sometimes would be too well bred to let it be seen that they felt superior to him because of their higher birth, but they would feel it and he would know that they felt it. He would always be conscious of being a parvenu in the social circles where his mother and her family moved. Almost against his will, she was leading him to eventual unhappiness and fame.

BIBLIOGRAPHY[26]

The correspondence of Gerard with Mlle du Motier is to be found in the University of Chicago Library, DC146, f. L2A3, Vol. I. Genealogical data regarding the Lafayette family are to be found in the Bibliothèque Nationale, manuscrits français 20229, fol. 158; 20242, fols. 1–3; 20262, fol. 13; and in "A collection of forty original manuscripts relating to the family antecedents of the Marquis de Lafayette" in the Manuscripts Division of the Library of Congress; see also Comte Georges de Morant, *Tableau de filiation de la maison du Motier de La Fayette avec l'état présent de la descendance du Général La Fayette* (Paris, 1928). On Lafayette's ancestors, in addition to the sources indicated in the footnotes, see Henri Doniol, "La famille, l'enfance et la première jeunesse du Marquis de La Fayette," in *Séances et travaux de l'Académie des Sciences Morales et Politiques*, CVI (1876), 171–95, also reprinted in revised form as chap. xix of Vol. I (pp. 651–70) of *La participation de la France à l'établissement des Etats Unis d'Amérique* (5 vols.; Paris, 1886–

[25] "Fayette" in Lachénaye-Desbois, *Dictionnaire de la noblesse* (Paris, 1773).

[26] These bibliographies are intended only to supplement the footnotes, which should also be consulted.

90). Albert Ojardias and Comte Jean de Pusy–La Fayette, *Pourquoi La Fayette s'appelait-il La Fayette?* (reprinted from *L'almanach de Brioude* [Brioude, 1933]) is highly inaccurate. The statement in the *Mémoires du Général Lafayette*, I, 90 n., and in Mme de Lasteyrie's *Vie de Madame de Lafayette* (Paris, 1869), p. 193 n., on the inheritance of Lafayette is also mistaken; cf. Doniol, *op. cit.*, pp. 653–54, and Mosnier, p. 13.

E. Charavay, *Le Général La Fayette, 1757–1834* (Paris, 1898), in addition to being, despite many more recent biographies, the best study of Lafayette's career, is valuable also for the Appendix and for the collection of *pièces justificatives* at the close of his book (pp. 531–99). Jules Cloquet, *Recollections of the private life of General Lafayette* (London, 1835), is by Lafayette's doctor and close personal friend. It is in the form of letters to Isaiah Townsend of Albany, New York. Mr. Townsend translates them, and his version, "which is more correct than the original" (p. viii), was published in the *New York Evening Star*. Messrs. A. L. W. Galigini et Cie published a French edition of them: *Souvenirs sur la vie privée du Général Lafayette* (Paris, 1836) from the original French letters "revised and corrected" by Cloquet himself. Cloquet was sometimes inaccurate, but never deliberately so.

On Lafayette's father, the fullest account is in *Mémoires autographes de M. le Prince de Montbarey* (3 vols.; Paris, 1826–27). The biography of La Colombe by Ulysse Rouchon contains some papers that belonged to La Colombe's father, who was a friend of the Lafayettes. These papers give some rather interesting and otherwise unknown details regarding Lafayette's earliest days. In the catalogue of the *Exposition du centenaire de La Fayette (1757–1834)*, arranged by André Girodie (Blérancourt, 1934), are described several unpublished documents that were in the possession of M. Emmanuel Fabius, autograph dealer of Paris; in 1964 they were divided between the Bibliothèque Nationale and the Cornell University Library, each getting the whole collection either in the originals or in microfilm.

CHAPTER II

Grooming a Courtier

ON THE left bank of the Seine, in the heart of the Latin Quarter of Paris, stands the Palais du Luxembourg. A huge block of buildings with its surrounding gardens, it marks the height of French Renaissance architecture and symbolizes the grandeur of the early Bourbon monarchy. Marie de' Medici once made her home in this palace, where now the austere Senate of France holds forth. In the eighteenth century it was nothing more than a sort of apartment house, in which lived the more favored nobles of the court who were not rich enough to have their own town houses. Here the Comte de La Rivière, Lafayette's great-grandfather, made his home, and it was here that Lafayette's mother now took him.

This was quite different from Chavaniac. The château in the Auvergne mountains had seemed enormous when viewed beside the little peasant houses close by, but compared to the Luxembourg Palace it looked dwarfed and provincial indeed. The rugged beauty of the Chavaniac hills appeared primitive after seeing the geometrically arranged trees, the formally planted flowers, the regularly placed statues of the spacious Luxembourg gardens. And here besides were men folk. First of all, there were his grandparents. His grandfather, the Marquis de La Rivière, had been one of the Breton nobles who had conspired against the Duc d'Orleans, regent during the minority of Louis XV. Forced to flee to Spain, the marquis had been mistaken for another gentleman and had spent a short period in prison. It was this exile and imprisonment which had kept him from a military career. It had not prevented him from amassing a fortune, however. He had a reputation for being a learned man and a very careful manager. He spent a large part of the year at his estate at Keroflais in Brittany, where he was generally believed to be an old miser. Nevertheless, as was to be discovered at his death, he had actually made many grants to charity.

The Marquis de La Rivière was not the son, but the son-in-law, of Lafayette's great-grandfather, the Comte de La Rivière. For the parents of Julie de La Rivière-Lafayette were cousins of the same family name. Unlike his son-in-law, the Comte de La Rivière, handsome and fond of society, had had a brilliant military career. He was now lieutenant-general in the king's armies, Grand Cross of the Royal and Military Order of St. Louis, and governor of Rocroy and other places.[1] Both the Comte and the Marquis de La Rivière were now widowers.[2]

In addition to his two grandparents, Gilbert met, at the Luxembourg apartment, the Comte de Lusignem, who was likewise a gentleman of rank and ancient lineage. Lusignem's first wife had been one of the Comte de La Rivière's daughters. Thus, because of the curious marriage of Lafayette's grandfather with his own cousin, the Comte de La Rivière's other daughter, Lusignem was both the brother-in-law and the cousin by marriage of Lafayette's grandfather, the Marquis de La Rivière. His relationship to Lafayette was therefore rather complicated. Now that both of the Comte de La Rivière's daughters were dead and the Comte de Lusignem had married again, the relationship was even more anomalous. But the Comte and the new Comtesse de Lusignem remained very close to the La Rivières. It was, in fact, the Lusignem's apartment at the Luxembourg in which they all lived. Lafayette came to regard them as his aunt and uncle and they looked upon him as a dearly beloved nephew. He also frequently saw his cousin, the Abbé de Murat, who had held him to the baptismal font. The abbé was now vicar-general of the archbishop of Paris. These men, dignitaries of both state and church, assumed responsibil-

---

[1] See a *bail*, done at Brioude, March 6, 1780, now to be found at the Lafayette Memorial, Inc., at Chavaniac; cf. Charavay, pp. 552–53.

[2] Cf. Luynes, *Mémoires*, XIII, 227; and "Autobiographie," Charavay, p. 533.

ity for him. But there was really no one to play with in his new
family. The Comte de Lusignem had a son by his first marriage,
who was therefore a cousin of Lafayette and who was one day
to share with him the estate of the Comte de La Rivière.[3] Yet
the two boys never developed a friendship.

Gilbert saw very little of his grandfather, for the old man was
frequently at Keroflais in Brittany, superintending his estate
and amassing a fortune with the penury and thrift for which he
became famous. His great-grandfather, who had recently retired
as commandant of the Second Company of the King's Musketeers, took charge of his education. A young nobleman just
entering upon his teens must go to school. His grandfather did
not have much confidence that he would make a good record,
but nevertheless picked out one of the most aristocratic of the
Paris educational institutions for him. This was the Collège du
Plessis. It stood not very far from the Palais du Luxembourg,
on the site now occupied by the newer part of the Lycée Louis-
le-Grand. The Sorbonne and the Collège de France flanked it on
either side, though they were of very little interest to a young
nobleman who was planning to embark upon a military career
as soon as possible. The Abbé Fayon had taught the young
marquis more than his grandfather had believed, for when the
lad was admitted he was found well enough advanced to enter
the fourth year.

Gilbert lived at the Collège du Plessis about four years. This
school was sometime later to have a few professors of unorthodox points of view, but Gilbert's generation was not exposed to
any such contamination. His training was entirely conventional. It consisted chiefly of Latin. This was the study most
emphasized in eighteenth-century France, and Lafayette had a
special aptitude for it. Before he finished, he won his college
prize for Latin composition and even tried for the more cov-
eted *prix d'université*. But there he had to meet the competi-
tion of older boys who had prepared themselves for the contest

3 Lafayette to M. Tripier, March 22, 1817, in J. P. Morgan Library, New York
City; cf. contract for sale of lands signed jointly by Lafayette and Lusignem, December
8, 1783, Morristown National Historical Park, Morristown, N.J.

by repeating the same courses two or three times. Nevertheless he thought it was only his carelessness in recopying his composition which cost him the prize. He had omitted an entire sentence and the grader had marked each word in the omitted sentence as a separate mistake. He was keenly disappointed, as he had felt confident of success and his friends had already congratulated him on his assured triumph. Even after he had become an old man he continued to feel that he had been the victim of a rank injustice.

His Latin studies placed among his heroes one who appealed to few of his generation—Vercingetorix, the Gaul who had defended his beloved Auvergne mountains against Julius Caesar. Hard by the château at Chavaniac there were some fields which the natives called the "Champs de Bataille," and they were believed to have been the scene of a bloody struggle between the Romans and the Gauls. Long afterward Lafayette hoped he had Gallic rather than Frankish blood in his veins. "I have a higher regard for Vercingetorix defending our mountains than for Clovis and his successors,"[4] he then said. But, in his adolescent years, like most of his contemporaries, he probably was taught to prefer Plutarch's galaxy of Greek and Roman exemplars to any of the Franks or Gauls. An affection for the barbarian Vercingetorix was somewhat unorthodox in the eighteenth-century classical tradition.

His favorite teacher at the Collège du Plessis was his instructor of French rhetoric. This was René Binet, who some years later became rector of the University of Paris and, after the French Revolution, principal of the Lycée Bonaparte. M. Binet recognized in the quiet lad a young man of spirit. One day Lafayette's class was required to write a composition on the perfect horse. The professor had in mind a well-disciplined animal which at the sight of a whip became perfectly obedient. Lafayette's composition, however, depicted as the perfect horse one that when threatened with a whip threw his rider and galloped off. M. Binet long remembered the composition, and when both

4 "Autobiographie," Charavay, p. 531.

teacher and pupil were old men, delighted to recall the episode.[5]
So did Lafayette, as proof that even as a child he had not considered submission to tyranny a token of perfection.

The whip as a means of inspiring perfect discipline was not
unknown at the Collège du Plessis. Despite their illustrious
families and their wealth, despite their embroidered clothes,
their powdered and pomaded hair, their queues in silken
pockets, and the swords at their sides, these young dandies of
the aristocracy were thoroughly subdued by their befrocked and
becassocked professors. The more spirited among the pupils
sometimes tried resistance; and Lafayette was one of these. He
had gained some ascendancy among his comrades and was soon
surrounded by his friends, most of them bigger than himself,
whenever he appeared in the school courtyard. Once when he
believed that one of his schoolmates had been unjustly pun-
ished, Gilbert felt called upon to raise rebellion among them.
He did not receive sufficient support, however, and the rebellion
failed. The youthful ringleader expected to be severely rebuked
and had determined to resist even at the point of the sword, but
tactful teachers allowed the incident to pass quietly. The young
man had to wait for martyrdom and glory. Yet he had begun
to be dimly aware of an idea which he was to announce to a
troubled world in the future—that resistance to oppression was
one of the "inalienable and imprescriptible" rights of mankind.

Lafayette made no abiding friends among his schoolmates.
A young man named Fouchet[6] was the only one of them whom
he ever afterward mentioned by name, and him only casually.
The four years Gilbert spent at the Collège du Plessis, close to
the home of his Paris relatives, were nevertheless a pleasant period in the young man's career. He recalled them in later life
with tenderness and pride. Nothing, he then said, had displeased him there except the prevailing spirit of dependence.[7]

[5] *Mémoires*, I, 8; "Autobiographie," Charavay, p. 536; and B. Sarrans, *Lafayette
et la Révolution de 1830: histoire des choses et des hommes de Juillet* (2 vols.; Brussels,
1832), II, 2.

[6] Lafayette to Major du Fouchet, General Gates's headquarters at the camp at
Whitemarsh, December 1, [1777], in the Lafayette College Library, Easton, Pa.

[7] Lafayette to M. le Chamberland d'Hennings, Wittmold, January 15, 1799, in Huntington Library, HM 21654; cf. *Mémoires*, III, 220.

The worst part of school was that the exiled pupil missed Chavaniac. He sometimes wrote home to his cousin, and the high spots in these years were the vacations. Two of them he spent in Auvergne with his grandmother, his aunts, and his beloved playmate. The long days on the dusty, bumpy roads in a lumbering coach were well rewarded by the sight of the home where he was master and head of the house. He told his cousin all about the people he met at Paris and about the balls and dinners that he sometimes attended with the great. They laughed together over the gossip about the capital's celebrities. When he had to return to Paris, he wrote to her about his Paris friends just as if she knew them as well as he, and poked fun at the huge new hats which the women of fashion were wearing and whose "contours and compartments" he said, could be described only "with compass in hand."[8] There was, after all, no one among the grown-ups at the Palais du Luxembourg, or even among the boys at school, with whom he could laugh like that.

Gilbert had been in school only about two years when a double tragedy came to narrow the tiny circle of his friends. He had come to love his mother very dearly. In the two years following his removal from Chavaniac they had been very close together, and he learned to admire her wit and her beauty. In the spring of 1770 she became very ill, and died at the Luxembourg Palace on April 3, not yet thirty-three years of age. The funeral took place the next day at the church of St. Sulpice, a stone's throw from the Palais. Only the broken-hearted son and his "uncle" Lusignem were present. Her father, the Marquis de La Rivière, despite his reputation for severity and harshness, died of grief for the last of his children a few weeks later. At the age of thirteen the Marquis de Lafayette was left without father or mother or grandfather. At Chavaniac his grandmother still survived and guarded his affairs. In Paris he was left to his "uncles" Lusignem and Murat, and his great-grandfather. The home at the Luxembourg Palace, suddenly bereft of his mother

---

[8] Lafayette to Mlle de Chavaniac, February 8, 1772, in *Mémoires*, I, 6–7, n. 4. The letter was in the possession of Emmanuel Fabius: see p. 15 above and Girodie, p. 14, no. 11.

and grandfather, was emptier than ever before. The Comtesse de Lusignem took his mother's place as well as she could, but away from Chavaniac the lad felt very much alone.

Still he was rich. The Marquis de La Rivière had left him a tidy fortune. At the age of thirteen he could expect, on attaining his majority, to have an annual income of 120,000 livres (about $240,000), instead of the 25,000 he had hitherto enjoyed. In addition to his old estates of La Fayette, Vissac, Siaugues–St. Romain, and Chavaniac, he had recently acquired those of Reignac, Kaufrait, St. Quihoelt, Le Plessis, La Touche, and other places. He was now a Breton noble, as well as an Auvergnat. None of the boys he knew was equally rich, even if some of them had prouder titles and more quarterings on their family escutcheons than his simple arms.[9]

The Comte de La Rivière decided that a rich nobleman of thirteen summers should have more to occupy him than mere schooling. It was time he began his military career. The comte had been captain-lieutenant and commandant of the Second Company of the King's Musketeers until his retirement in 1766, and Gilbert's mother's brother before his premature death had served in the same regiment. The young heir to the La Rivière fortune must continue the family tradition. The proper steps were taken, and on April 9, 1771, Lafayette entered his grandparent's company as one of the proud Black Musketeers. It was the regiment that Alexandre Dumas was one day to make famous.

Lafayette was still a schoolboy burning to wear a uniform. It was a great experience for him to be excused from classes in order to dress up for parades and reviews. But the greatest thrill of all was to be allowed one day in full regimentals to ride his horse from headquarters in Paris to the palace at Versailles in order to ask the king whether he had any orders for the Musketeers. This was a ceremony that was performed every day of the year and invariably resulted in the king's bored reply that

---

[9] Gules, band of or, and bordure of vair; motto: *Vis sat contra fatum* ("Vigor suffices against fate").

he had no orders to give. But Lafayette never forgot the pride with which he brought back to his commandant the impressive message that Louis XV had repeated for that day.

Thus, amid tragedies, parades, and the daily routine of school life, Lafayette ceased to be a child. He was close to fourteen years of age. He had a huge income and had begun a promising military career. Among his relatives were men of influence and prestige. He had not completely lost his country manner, he was still shy and awkward, and his sandy hair, receding forehead, and large nose did not proclaim him a fashionable beauty. But an income of 120,000 livres a year with no relatives to share it would counterbalance any personal shortcomings he might have. He was a good match, and a good bride must be found for him.

Officious friends of the family had already been actively engaged as matchmakers. M. de La Colombe, a neighbor of Chavaniac, assuming the privilege that long acquaintance with Gilbert's grandmother gave him, decided that the only surviving scion of an illustrious Auvergne house must be married as soon as nature would allow. Lafayette was not yet fourteen years old when this zealous well-wisher began to cast his eye among the eligible young ladies of the French aristocracy. It fell approvingly upon Mlle de Crussol, daughter of the late minister of Louis XV to the court of Parma. She was rather short and homely, but spirited and intelligent. Though her fortune was small, her family's influence at court would be worth more than livres to a young Auvergnat squire. The Vicomtesse de Crussol was not opposed to the marriage, but she did wonder whether her daughter was not too mature for the marquis. The young lady was nineteen years of age, almost six years older than her proposed husband.

M. de La Colombe did not consider this difference in age important. If young Gilbert did not make his wife happy, he said, he would be the first of his family to fail in this regard. The well-meaning matchmaker even thought that the greater maturity of the prospective bride might be a distinct advantage to the lad. Having neither father nor mother, should he lose his aged grandmother, "it would be essential for him that his wife be older." M. de La Colombe intended to see the Marquise de Lafayette and, as a friend of both the houses involved, place the matter before her.[10]

Nothing ever came out of this proposal. Nevertheless, the desirability of finding a mate for the orphaned heir of the Lafayettes was apparent and occupied the family's attention all during the following year.[11] Finally, during Gilbert's second vacation in the beloved Chavaniac hills, shortly before his fifteenth birthday, his great-grandfather arranged his marriage into the illustrious Noailles family.[12]

When Gilbert returned in the summer of 1772 to take up his abode at the Luxembourg Palace, he left behind him a childhood which differed little in significance from most childhoods. Except that he was orphaned, and away from Chavaniac, very much alone, his tragedies and joys, triumphs and failures, had not been great or enduring. Yet he was fondly to recall those years as a time when he had been happy. The ones that were immediately to follow were not to be so pleasant. When the young lord rode away from the towers of his provincial home, he saw his family together for the last time. Ten years later he came back a famous man, but only the widowed, childless Mme de Chavaniac was left to welcome him. Soon after his departure his grandmother died. His cousin married and succumbed in childbirth, and his Aunt du Motier, though she lived to hear of his success, ended her career before his triumphant return to the Auvergne mountains.

---

[10] M. de Jouy to M. de La Colombe, [spring, 1771], and M. de La Colombe to M. de Jouy, April 1, 1771, Rouchon, *La Colombe*, pp. 9–11.

[11] It is possible that the "cousin" and "nephew" whose proposed marriage to Mlle de Roncherolles is discussed in Lafayette's letter to his cousin, February 8, 1772 (*Mémoires*, I, 6–7, n. 4) is Lafayette himself.

[12] Lafayette (Charavay, p. 536) says he learned of this while still at Chavaniac, but see below, p. 28.

BIBLIOGRAPHY

See bibliography for chap. i.

Sarrans, *Lafayette et la Révolution de 1830* (2 vols.; Brussels, 1832) was written as an apology for Lafayette by one of his aides-de-camp. The information for the career of Lafayette before 1830 was furnished largely by Lafayette himself, whom Sarrans had known and revered since childhood. For the details regarding the death of Lafayette's mother, see "Lafayette" in A. Jal, *Dictionnaire critique de biographie et d'histoire* (Paris, 1867). H. Doniol, *Établissement des États-Unis*, I, 660 n., confuses the two La Rivières in a mistaken effort to correct Lafayette's *Mémoires*. Michel de La Bedoyère, "Lafayette and the church," *Catholic world*, CXXXIX (1934), 166–70, contains some interesting details, but gratuitously assumes that Lafayette's education was unorthodox; cf. Daniel Mornet, *Les origines intellectuelles de la Révolution française (1715–1787)* (Paris, 1933), pp. 175, 330–31, 398–99.

CHAPTER III

A Good Match

I T WAS the Duc d'Ayen who decided upon the young Marquis de Lafayette for a son-in-law. He had no sons and five daughters, and good catches like the marquis were none too plentiful. D'Ayen had much to offer on his own side. Above all, he was a Noailles. Both his great-grandfather and his grandfather had been marshals of France, and it was only a question of time until his father, the present Duc de Noailles, should also become one. That gentleman at one time had been a second-string lover of Mme de Vintimille, the king's mistress,[1] and was now a famous general. In the Seven Years' War, he had made a reputation for himself as a cautious, even timorous, fighter. Once, when this worthy had come close to falling out of a boat, the Duc d'Ayen chided the servants with a *bon mot* that reached the ears of Horace Walpole: "Don't you know that my father fears water as much as fire?"[2] The Duc de Noailles' brother, the Comte de Noailles, better known as the Duc de Mouchy, was also a prominent soldier. The Noailles had good reason to be one of the proudest families of France. When John Adams visited them in 1778 he was informed that they had become "more powerful than the House of Bourbon."[3]

The Duc d'Ayen was himself a gentleman of considerable importance. He had a reputation as a wit and as a scientist. He already held a high rank in the army, and was designated to

[1] D'Argenson, *Journal et mémoires*, III, 383–85 (under date of September 5, 1741); cf. Georg Brandes, *Voltaire* (2 vols.; New York, 1930) I, 283.

[2] Walpole to the Rev. William Mason, April 5, 1777, in the *Letters of Horace Walpole*, ed. Mrs. Paget Toynbee, X, *1777–1779*, 36.

[3] Charles Francis Adams (ed.), *The works of John Adams*, III (Boston, 1851), 149–50.

follow his father as governor of the king's Château of St. Germain, captain of the King's Bodyguard, and governor of the province of Roussillon. He had, moreover, married the granddaughter of the Chancellor d'Aguesseau, one of the greatest ministers and most honest jurists of Louis XV's reign. Surely such a man need not seek far or long for a qualified son-in-law.[4]

D'Ayen's daughters were still very young. Adrienne, the second of them, was only twelve years of age when her father began seriously to look around for husbands for her and her older sister. About the same time the Comte de La Rivière and the Comtesse de Lusignem were searching for a wife for the Marquis de Lafayette. The great-granddaughter of the Chancellor d'Aguesseau and granddaughter of the Duc de Noailles would be a splendid catch for the young country squire, and his large income was very persuasive to the Duc d'Ayen. The duke decided to talk it over with his wife.

Much to his chagrin, the Duchess d'Ayen hesitated. She had always been a pious and faithful mother, and since her recovery from a bad attack of the smallpox and the death of her infant son, she had become especially devoted to her daughters. She was loath to part from them or to see their education interrupted so soon. Though all she could learn of the proposed son-in-law's personality was in his favor, she saw good arguments against the match in his youth, his excessive fortune, and his isolation. The more D'Ayen argued, the more stubborn she became. For several months they quarreled over the question. Her husband knew, however, that she would eventually listen to reason. "You don't know Mme d'Ayen," he said one day. "No matter how far she may go, you may rest assured that she will come back like a child, if you prove to her that she is wrong, but, on the other hand, she will never yield, if she does not see it."[5] He finally won her over to his point of view by promising that the marriage would be postponed for two years, and that

---

[4] See *Almanach royal* for 1772; also Anonymous, *Anne-Paule-Dominique de Noailles, Marquise de Montagu* (Paris, 1872), pp. 6–7.

[5] Mme de Lafayette, "Notice sur la vie de sa mère, Mme. la Duchesse d'Ayen," in Mme de Lasteyrie, *Vie de Madame de Lafayette*, p. 43.

in the meantime young Lafayette's education would be completed.

Since the elder of the two marriageable daughters was a little too old for Lafayette, it was decided that she should become betrothed to her cousin, the Vicomte de Noailles, while the younger Adrienne should be promised to the marquis from Auvergne. The Duc d'Ayen and his wife reached this decision on September 21, 1772. Lafayette had just turned fifteen years of age.[6] Adrienne d'Ayen (b. November 2, 1759) was not yet thirteen. The two girls knew that their father and mother had disagreed about something, but they did not know what it was. Their joy was none the less sincere when the reconciliation of their parents took place. They were still kept in ignorance about the match, however.

The affection of the young people for each other was the least important point to be considered. The details of the marriage contract had to be arranged, and they took skilful handling. A tentative contract was drawn up in October, immediately after the Duchesse d'Ayen gave her consent to the marriage. The prospective groom was informed by his great-grandfather of the destined alliance shortly thereafter. He seemed "quite content," the Comte de La Rivière informed the young man's aunt at Chavaniac.[7] The final terms of the contract still required several months of delicate negotiations. There were so many interests to be taken into account. The D'Aguesseaus, the Noailles, the La Rivières, the Lafayettes all had to be consulted and all were in some way or other parties to the arrangement. The daughter of one of the most influential houses in France could not marry one of the country's richest young men without a carefully prepared document agreed to by all concerned. Now that Lafayette's grandmother was dead, Lafayette's closest pa-

[6] In the "Autobiographie," Lafayette says fourteen years of age (cf. Charavay, p. 536), but this is an error.

[7] Comte de La Rivière to Mlle du Motier, November 13, 1772, in the collection of Emmanuel Fabius: see p. 15 above and Girodie, p. 14, no. 12. The *projet de contrat de mariage* of October, 1772, is described *ibid.*, pp. 15–16, no. 14. For the details given below regarding the negotiation of the final marriage contract, see the letter of the Abbé de Murat to his "chère cousine" [Mlle du Motier], Paris, February 12, 1773, in the Lafayette Memorial, Inc., at Chavaniac.

ternal relatives were his two aunts at Chavaniac. They intrusted
the entire matter to the Abbé de Murat, their cousin, and
Gerard, the lawyer.

Mme d'Ayen's insistence that Adrienne know nothing of what
was going on added to the complications. The matchmakers
could seldom meet at the Noailles home for their consultations,
and had to use the Lusignems' Luxembourg apartment instead.
Nevertheless it was all slowly arranged. Adrienne was kept in
complete darkness. Lafayette, who now lived with the Lusignems, sometimes was present at the discussions of the contract
but never interposed any difficulties. It was agreed that
Adrienne should have a dowry of 400,000 livres, but there was
some question as to the source of this sum. Mme d'Ayen had
promised it out of her own dowry, and it was found that certain
conditional statements in her marriage contract made such a
settlement difficult. She had been pledged 1,500,000 livres by
her father for her oldest son, or, if there were no male heirs, for
the daughter of her choice. Mme d'Ayen had at first intended
to divide this sum equally among all of her daughters, making
a dowry of about 300,000 livres for each of them, but M.
d'Aguesseau objected. He even threatened to disinherit his
daughter if she annulled this clause of her marriage contract.

The Abbé de Murat began to wonder whether the sum promised his ward would ever be secured. At a conference at the
Comte de La Rivière's one day in February, 1773, he asked to
see the D'Ayen marriage contract. It was presented for his examination the next day at their notary's office. Murat was convinced that the terms of the contract made the 1,500,000 livres
in question too uncertain a source for Adrienne's dowry, and
requested a statement of Mme d'Ayen's other assets. After five
hours at the notary's office he discovered that the duchesse was
worth nearly 2,000,000 livres in her own right in addition to the
1,500,000 of D'Aguesseau's. That satisfied him.

It was at first agreed that the formal witnessing of the contract should take place at the D'Ayen's home in the Noailles
hôtel, but this would have involved Adrienne's being informed,
and Mme d'Ayen was not yet ready for that step. So when the

Abbé de Murat arrived at the Noailles', he was asked to go to the home of M. d'Aguesseau. There he found the Duc and Duchesse d'Ayen, the Duchesse de Noailles, and M. and Mme d'Aguesseau, representing the bride, and the Comte de La Rivière, Mme de Lusignem, and Gerard representing the groom. Other legal and business men were also present. So was Lafayette. All of the young couple's relations signed the contract. Murat, however, signed only as the proxy of his cousin, Mlle du Motier, Lafayette's aunt. The king had graciously promised to affix his signature some time during the following September, and special permission had been secured for the others to do so before His Majesty.

Everybody was pleased. The only thing that marred the occasion at all was that Adrienne still knew nothing about it. Murat tried to make Mme d'Ayen acknowledge the difficulty of keeping her daughter in ignorance of a marriage which, he said, "had become so public that even the bootblacks were talking about it." Mme d'Ayen almost yielded, but in the end would consent only to things being done as if Mlle d'Ayen had really signed. On the first opportunity Murat wrote Lafayette's aunt all about what had taken place. "The essential thing," he said, "is that your nephew's mortgage [the 400,000 livres] dates from yesterday. . . . . If M. de Lafayette is getting a good bargain, Messrs. de Noailles are getting a better one for their girl. . . . . I have not yet seen Madame your future niece, neither has M. le Comte de La Rivière. Mde. la Duchesse d'Ayen has promised that I shall see her the first time I visit her. They tell me that she has a very pretty face." A mortgage of 400,000 livres with a pretty face thrown in really was *une affaire agréable*. But, despite Murat's precaution, for some reason or other, the *dot* was never paid in full.[8]

As good measure, Lafayette acquired a new home out of the bargain. It was arranged that the boy should go to live at the Noailles hôtel in Versailles. He was to return every other week

[8] Mme Lafayette to Gouverneur Morris, [May 29, 1802], in Huntington Library, HM 9451; Mme Lafayette indicates here that only 200,000 livres were actually received, but does not explain why.

and spend Sunday and Monday with his relatives in Paris.
Murat sent along with him a housekeeper who had been in his
own employ six years, and who, he was sure, would take good
care of the young marquis in his new quarters. Lafayette actually went off to live at Versailles the Monday after the contract
was signed (February 15, 1773). Thus once more the lad was
shunted around. From boarding school he had gone to his
"uncle" Lusignem's apartment, and from there he was now to
remove to the Noailles' house. Despite his wealth, he was not
to have a home of his own in Paris or Versailles until he was the
head of a growing family. For this state of affairs his grandfather's thrift and his great-grandfather's penury had been responsible, and to those circumstances was now added his intended mother-in-law's caution. On those occasions when the
D'Ayen family went to live in the Versailles hôtel, he was to
share the same roof with the girl he knew he was going to marry,
but his household was separate and he saw her only when her
mother was present, or when she was out for a walk. The Vicomte de Noailles, being the cousin of his intended bride, saw
somewhat more of Adrienne's older sister, and both affairs
prospered. Little Adrienne became completely enamored of the
orphan marquis from the country. Her devout mother evident-
ly understood the ways of the adolescent heart very well.

The removal of Lafayette to Versailles necessitated a change
in schooling. After four years at the Collège du Plessis a young
man who was intended for the army could get very little more
there to fit him for his future career. It was desirable that he
should complete his education in a manner becoming a young
noble of the sword. The Abbé Fayon was retained as a member
of his ménage, but a former army officer named Margelay was
added to the household. Margelay heard his lessons and taught
him practical things as well—particularly military matters.
Young Lafayette also learned the gentlemanly art of horseman-
ship at the riding academy of Versailles, where the aristocracy
of the court frequently sent their children. The Comte d'Artois,
the dauphin's younger brother, who was about the same age as

Lafayette, was one of its pupils.[9] Here the Marquis de Lafayette first came to know the future king of France, and some
of the highest-born noblemen of Versailles society. This was
quite unlike the Collège du Plessis. He was now at an age when
other people's rank and station seemed terribly impressive, and
the realization of his own recent lineage rendered him self-
conscious and maladroit. His recent rapid growth did not diminish his gaucherie. His awkwardness in every kind of gym-
nastic sport amused his companions. The Comte d'Artois, having no inhibitions himself and unable to understand the boy's
mental torture, thought him especially diverting. But the young
Auvergnat preserved his good nature and his academy mates
rather liked him.

The Duc d'Ayen meanwhile used his influence at court to
advance his young protégé's career. A Noailles must be more
than a King's Musketeer. He ought to serve in the Noailles
Dragoons. The ink was hardly dry on the marriage contract
of Lafayette when the Duc d'Ayen wrote to the Marquis de
Monteynard, minister of war, asking him to grant to the Marquis de Lafayette a commission as lieutenant in the Noailles
regiment. The Marquis de Monteynard hesitated, however, because Lafayette was only fifteen years of age, and there had
been three other lieutenants recently appointed in the same
corps. D'Ayen went personally to see Monteynard, explained
the particular reasons he had for wishing Lafayette's advance,
and confirmed this conversation in a second written request.[10]
The petition was granted. On April 7 Lafayette became a lieutenant in the Noailles cavalry. The war office could not easily
disregard the wishes of the Noailles, especially with regard to
promotion in a regiment over which they had certain proprietary
and traditional rights.

It was almost another year before the young lieutenant's
courtship of Mlle d'Ayen reached the point where the young lady

[9] Lafayette to unknown, La Grange, October 1, 1828, in Charavay, p. 458; *Mémoires*,
VI, 279; "Journal de Dumont d'Urbville," August 20, 1830, in Ach. de Vaulabelle,
Histoire des deux Restaurations, VII (Paris, 1857), 473.

[10] Duc d'Ayen to Marquis de Monteynard, Versailles, February 15 and March 7,
1773, A.M.G., dossier 1261.

fully understood what was going on. During the autumn of
1773 her older sister and the Vicomte de Noailles were married.
It was only several months afterward that Adrienne was told
of her own betrothal. The Duchess d'Ayen chose a fitting occasion to impart the secret. The several captains of the King's
Bodyguard served a quarter of each year at Versailles, and the
service of the Duc de Noailles and the Duc d'Ayen took place
annually during the winter months. It was at this period in
1774, when the D'Ayen family and their prospective son-in-law
were together at the court, that Mme d'Ayen decided to inform
her daughter of her engagement. Now, after almost two years
of ignorance, Adrienne first learned why her mother and father
had quarreled and why the Marquis de Lafayette had come to
live at their hôtel in Versailles. For over a year, the duchesse
explained, she had looked upon the young lieutenant as her son
and he was ready to regard her as a mother. He was a good
boy and he would make Adrienne happy, she said. The daughter was elated. Where children in their teens were married off
by the arrangements of their families, she was a lucky girl indeed who had been given a chance to develop an interest in the
man who had been chosen for her to marry. During the next
four months Adrienne readily learned the lessons the Duchesse
d'Ayen gave her and joined in her mother's prayers for success
in the new rôle she would soon be called upon to play.[11]

It was now the spring of 1774. Adrienne was not quite fourteen and a half years old. Gilbert was just sixteen and a half.
It was time they got married. The wedding was at first fixed for
the Sunday after Easter. In February, Lafayette's financial administrator, Gerard, had begun to prepare a report of Lafayette's properties as of April 1, 1774, for only such property
of the marquis as was expressly stipulated in the marriage contract was to become the common possession of the new pair,
and it was desirable for all concerned to know what his other
properties were. It was no easy task, as it involved getting ac-
curate reports and accounts from several widely scattered
points in France, at a time when transportation was no faster

[11] Mme de Lafayette, loc. cit., pp. 46–49.

than a horse could gallop.[12] The account was not completed when the wedding took place.

In fact, the difficulty of communication was so great that it almost caused a postponement of the ceremony. A record that Lafayette had been duly baptized was necessary before the wedding could be celebrated. Well beforehand Gerard had sent for an extract of this baptismal certificate, but Mlle du Motier had been absent, and at the end of March the necessary document had not yet arrived. Gerard wrote to the curé of Chavaniac begging him to send the desired record. Three days later he wrote again, more urgently. He also sent the bans of the wedding to be published in the parish of Chavaniac. It was not necessary, he said, to do this, but it would please Mlle du Motier.[13] In Paris the bans were published at the church of St. Roch, the bride's parish, and the church of St. Sulpice, the groom's, as well as that of Notre Dame at Versailles.

The wedding was finally celebrated on Monday, April 11, 1774. It took place in the chapel of the Noailles hôtel at Paris. The Abbé de Murat, who had held Lafayette at the baptismal font, performed the ceremony. Witnessing for the groom were the Comte de Lusignem, as his maternal great-uncle, and the Marquis de Bouillé, who had married the late Marquise de Lafayette's sister and was therefore his paternal great-uncle. Witnessing for the bride were the Duc de Mouchy, her great-uncle, and the Comte de Tessé, her uncle. The Comte de La Rivière, the Comte de Lusignem, Murat, and Gerard, on the groom's side, and the Duc and Duchesse de Noailles, the Duc and Duchesse d'Ayen, and the Vicomte de Noailles, on the bride's, also signed the marriage act. So too did the bride and the groom, who designated himself as "du Motier de Lafayette," in a characteristic "small and quite bad handwriting."[14]

[12] Gerard to Mlle du Motier, Paris, February 23; May 15; July 1; December 28, 1774; November 25, 1775, in University of Chicago Library, DC 146 f. L2A3, Vol. I. See also below, pp. 61–62.

[13] Gerard to the curé of Chavaniac, Paris, March 25 and 28, 1774, University of Chicago Library, DC 146 f. L2A3, Vol. I.

[14] "Lafayette" in A. Jal, *Dictionnaire critique de biographie et d'histoire* (Paris, 1867), p. 721; "Lafayette" in *Le curieux*, II (1886), 123–27; Charavay, pp. 556–59.

It was a great event for Paris society. For some days thereafter the Comte de La Rivière and the Comte de Lusignem were kept busy calling on people and leaving formal announcements of the wedding.[15] But for the young bridegroom his marriage had been the occasion of another affront to his family. The royal genealogist had, about a month before the ceremony, seen fit to ask him for his titles of nobility. If, like the Noailles, he had been included in the recently published *Dictionnaire de la noblesse* (1773), this would have been unnecessary. The young country squire replied haughtily that he considered his family so well known that he did not need to prove his titles. The genealogist had therefore to be content, when Louis XV demanded to see the papers of the man who was marrying into the august Noailles family, to put before His Majesty a letter written in 1762 to the king on the occasion of the presentation of Lafayette's mother at court. Once more Lafayette owed his social standing to his mother rather than to his father's ancestors.[16]

The newlyweds remained at the hôtel of the Noailles in Paris. It was situated at what was then 235 Rue St. Honoré. Its gardens, one of the beauty spots of Paris, ran all the way to the gates of the Tuileries Palace. Part of it was later destroyed to make room for the Rue d'Alger. What remains is now the Hôtel de St. James et Albany; other buildings have crowded around it to shut it off from the street.[17] It lay in the fashionable Faubourg St. Honoré in the parish of St. Roch, whose baroque church, only a minute's walk away on the same street, still stands, barely changed in recent centuries. Here the *acte de mariage* of the young couple was duly registered.

Lafayette was now a Noailles. He was married to a Noailles,

[15] Bib. Nat., Français 27603, pièces originales 1119, fol. 72; facsimile in Charavay, between pp. 4 and 5. On April 30, the Duc d'Ayen wrote to Lafayette's aunt, congratulating himself on his "new acquisition" in the person of her nephew (Girodie, p. 26, no. 35).

[16] Chérin, the royal genealogist, to the Duc de La Vrillière, Paris, March 12, 1774, in Charavay, pp. 556 n.

[17] *Marquise de Montagu*, p. 6 and note; François Boucher and Francis Wilson Huard, *American footprints in Paris* (New York, 1921), pp. 116–17.

he lived in their house, he contributed 8,000 livres a year to the household expenses,[18] he served in their regiment, he called the duc and the duchesse "papa" and "mama." But he was going to find that he did not altogether like it.

BIBLIOGRAPHY

The biography of Adrienne de Noailles-Lafayette's sister, *Anne-Paule-Dominique de Noailles, Marquise de Montagu* (Paris, 1872), though anonymous, is by her children; its chief significance for the life of Lafayette before 1777 is that it confirms Mme de Lafayette's account of her mother in Lasteyrie, *Madame de Lafayette*.

[18] Charavay, p. 5, n. 3.

CHAPTER IV

A Frustrated Courtier

O F ALL the Noailles family, the Duc d'Ayen, oldest of
the second generation of living Noailles, was the most
popular. Mme d'Ayen, however, was of a more retiring
disposition, and, besides, had had five girls to look after and to
educate. She had long been content to let her husband's aunt,
the Comtesse de Noailles—"Mme Etiquette," as the dauphiness
called her—take the lead in Versailles society, and an invitation
to the comtesse's ball was generally considered a most distinguished honor. But now that two of her daughters were married, Mme d'Ayen tried to play the part in the social world that
she felt she owed to them and to their husbands. Through her
solicitude young Lafayette soon met everyone at court that it
was important for him to know and found himself one of a
brilliant circle of pleasure-seeking young bloods.

When Lafayette's marriage took place, Louis XV was still
king of France. During the aged ruler's last years, court society
had been constantly involved in intrigue and scandal. Many of
the more sedate ladies of the aristocracy disapproved of the
king's open relations with Mme du Barry. The former cour-
tesan, whom a doting monarch had raised to the nobility and
who sometimes determined offhand royal policies which wiser
but less attractive heads found it hard to understand, scandalized the court by her bad manners and indecorous behavior.
On Lafayette, who knew only women like his aunt and his
mother-in-law, Mme du Barry made an indelible impression.
He had encountered her on several different occasions, even before his wedding. One day he saw Louis XV and his mistress
playing cards, and was struck by the king's embarrassment at

Mme du Barry's unconventionality when she lost.[1] The expression she used was harmless enough but definitely slangy, and vulgarity was almost the only unpardonable offense one could commit at Louis XV's Versailles.

Into this society young Lafayette did not exactly fit. It made him feel out of his element and ill at ease. He began to take refuge from it in silence and introspective brooding. Shortly after he and Adrienne were married, he was present at the Trianon Palace when the king and his favorite were having dinner together. Louis suddenly fell ill with what proved to be the attack of smallpox which carried him off about two weeks later (May 10, 1774).[2] All the court spoke of this misadventure with great agitation. But young Lafayette, timid and reticent, said not a word about it to anyone. When the Noailles learned what had happened, they were amazed at his seeming nonchalance, and he gained an unenviable reputation as a stolid and phlegmatic young man. Only those who knew him best— his wife and her kindly mother—saw that underneath the increasingly reserved exterior there was hidden a warm, excitable nature.

Not even the death of a king could long delay the rewards that the marriage of the taciturn marquis to the daughter of the Noailles was expected to bring. Three months before the wedding had taken place the Duc d'Ayen had begun to solicit another promotion for the young lieutenant of the Noailles cavalry. The Prince de Poix, Mouchy's eldest son and D'Ayen's cousin-german, was expected some day to become one of the colonels of the Noailles Dragoons. The Prince de Poix was already a captain in the regiment, and when his promotion took place, D'Ayen felt that Lafayette ought to have the captaincy which his cousin would thus vacate. He wrote a letter to the minister of war to this effect, but Monteynard, on this occasion, as on the previous promotion of Lafayette, hesitated because of the candidate's youth. For the marquis was only sixteen years

---

[1] Cloquet, p. 270; cf. *Mémoires de B. Barère* (Paris, 1844), IV, 277–78.

[2] Cloquet, p. 270; cf. Doniol, *Histoire de la participation de la France à l'établissemen des États-Unis*, I, 664 n., which tells a different story.

old. The minister was willing, however, that the captaincy remain vacant until the boy became of age to fill it.

This was before the wedding. After his daughter's marriage to Lafayette, the Duc d'Ayen opened the question again. Lafayette was now only a few months older, but the Duc d'Ayen again, as on the earlier occasion, urged "particular reasons" of a private nature which he did not specify, for wishing that Lafayette's promotion might become effective at once. The actual commission, D'Ayen argued, need not be delivered to Lafayette, but might remain undated in the war-department files until he reached his eighteenth birthday. All that D'Ayen asked was a letter instructing him, as the present commanding officer of the Noailles regiment, to make such an arrangement. Precedents existed for such a procedure, D'Ayen insisted, and cited the example of the young Comte de La Marck, one of his son-in-law's friends, who had been named colonel of the La Marck regiment with the proviso that he would assume actual command when he reached the age of twenty-three. The argument was convincing. Lafayette was appointed to the head of the company left vacant by the Prince de Poix's promotion, and actually received his commission, though it distinctly stipulated that he was to take charge of the company only upon reaching his eighteenth birthday.[3] This conditional promotion, however, did not prevent his having all the honors and prerogatives of his new rank. Thus, when he was only sixteen, his record of service at the war-department office read, "May 19, 1774: Captain." Through no merit of his own and simply because his father-in-law was exceptionally influential at Versailles, Lafayette was making a flying start on a promising military career.

This was not because the youthful captain's father-in-law thought very highly of him. On the contrary, the Duc d'Ayen sometimes spoke harshly to him, and he was always a little afraid of the older man. The duke considered him rather backward and not nearly as enterprising as his other son-in-law, the Vicomte de Noailles. But a young Noailles needed no special pushing, whereas a member of the new branch of Lafayettes,

[3] D'Ayen to Monteynard, January 11 and April 27, 1774, A.M.G., dossier 1261.

despite his fortune, might easily be overlooked if not vigorously prodded ahead.

Lafayette's regiment, the Noailles Dragoons, was part of the Army of the East, whose headquarters were at Metz. France, worn out by her defeats in the Seven Years' War and by internal quarrels between rival factions at court, had been at peace for more than ten years. This was the longest interval between wars in over a century. Louis XVI, whose reign had just begun, seemed to be intent upon domestic reform and amity with foreign nations. Yet the army must keep up its training, and Captain Lafayette had to leave his wistful bride and go off to Metz for the summer maneuvers.

The Vicomte de Noailles was also a captain in the same regiment. The two young men had become very close friends. Noailles was a dashing, brilliant officer, hard rider, hard drinker, hard gambler, and a leader among the younger set at court. Lafayette was only five months his junior, but worshiped him with the admiration of a timid adolescent for a bolder comrade. At Metz, Lafayette made the acquaintance also of Théodore de Lameth, the nephew of the commanding general and one of his aides,[4] and other young soldiers. But no warm bonds of friendship developed among them.

It was not until September that Lafayette returned from the summer maneuvers to his lonesome bride. He immediately determined upon a courageous act. The death of the old king from smallpox had put fear in the hearts of many of the nobility. In recent years there had been introduced into France from England, along with horse racing, heavy drinking, whist, and other importations, a process known as inoculation. By deliberately exposing one's self to a mild attack of smallpox, it was found possible to avoid more serious cases afterward. Because of the inexpertness of the physicians, however, there were involved the chance of becoming more than slightly ill and the risk of infection. It was a much more dangerous process than that of vaccination, which Dr. Jenner was at that moment engaged in per-

---

[4] Bib. Nat., nouvelles acquisitions françaises 1387, fols. 134–35; cf. *Mémoires de Théodore de Lameth*, ed. Eugène Welvert (Paris, 1913), pp. 104–5.

fecting, but of which no one in France had as yet heard. Inoculation required great courage or desperation, and religious scruples sometimes confirmed fear, for some claimed that to try to circumvent the ravages of the disease was an unwarranted interference with the ways of the Lord.

Lafayette, nevertheless, decided to risk it. His devoted little wife, who had never had the disease, determined, despite the possibility of contagion, to help him as much as she could, and so did her mother, whose gentle face was still disfigured from the attack which she had suffered. They rented a little house in Chaillot, on the outskirts of Paris, and there shut themselves up while the young husband underwent inoculation. It was a success. The intimacy of the little house at Chaillot, moreover, afforded the young couple a better opportunity to strengthen the affection that had sprung up between them than had been presented by the big city house of the Noailles, the many social functions that the Duc d'Ayen's family were obliged to attend, and the separation necessitated by military duties. Adrienne never forgot the happy days at Chaillot, but they were soon crowded out of her husband's mind by more important matters.

On their return to the city the young Lafayettes went to play their part at court. Under Louis XV the tone of society had been dictated by the older set. It was, if not austere, at least slow and even and traditional. The new king, Louis XVI, was an easy-going, stolid sort of person, painfully conscious of a physical deficiency which was the subject of general gossip around the town and which made him less robust than his younger brothers and his wife, Marie Antoinette. The young queen loved to dance, to play cards, to amuse herself. The retiring nature of her husband threw her more and more into the society of her brothers-in-law and particularly that of the younger of them, the Comte d'Artois, whose actions sometimes scandalized the court. The friendship of the queen and the prince became so notorious that when finally Marie Antoinette fulfilled her purpose on earth by giving birth to a child after about eight years of marriage, some libellists, not knowing or pretending not to know that the king had finally yielded to his surgeon, spread vague rumors abroad about the Comte d'Artois. Even earlier such gossip was not unheard. It interfered very little, however, with the activity of the youthful set of which the two were the leaders.

In this set the young people of the Noailles family played a conspicuous part. The Vicomte de Noailles, the Marquis de La-fayette, and their wives were frequently seen in the company of the queen and her dashing brother-in-law, along with the scions of other most illustrious families. The queen's balls were especially important events as they had ceased entirely during the merry widowerhood of the late monarch. The Duchesse d'Ayen went to particular pains to accompany her daughters to these affairs every week during the winter of 1775. She would also invite their young friends to her home for supper after the ball, and often the more intimate of them to her dinners. She soon acquired a reputation as a hostess which rivaled that of her aunt, the Comtesse de Noailles. Her lack of affectation, her natural goodness, and her charm made an invitation to her home a much-coveted distinction.

Despite the duchess' care, her sons-in-law became involved in all sorts of scrapes. They were ringleaders in the effort of the younger set to reintroduce into court the men's styles of the Henry IV period. There was a little method in this madness, as it was part of the revolt against the domination of the older gen-eration. The plumes, silk cloaks, ribbons, and bright colors of the Henrician costumes sat very well on a good-looking youth, but made a graceless, short, or thin old man appear slightly ridiculous. The queen joined the conspiracy and announced that the men who came to her balls must wear only this cos-tume. The younger courtiers were jubilant, and the older ones irate. But it was a short-lived victory, since the fad disappeared in the following summer, when the younger men went off to their army posts again.[5]

There were other newer fashions introduced by the younger set that were less innocent. Many of the pastimes of the Eng-

[5] Comte de Ségur, *Mémoires ou souvenirs et anecdotes* (3 vols.; Paris, 1825), I, 39-42; [Bachaumont], *Mémoires secrets*, XXIX, 339 (under date of January 24, 1775).

lish sporting world were then coming into vogue among the French. The Comte d'Artois was particularly fond of horse racing, and brought the race track with its attendant betting into France. Lafayette owned a good string of horses, though he was not a particularly accomplished rider. It was the Vicomte de Noailles who was the best equestrian of the group, and Lafayette was always glad to let him have the pick of his stables. Artois also indulged in card playing and was frequently a heavy loser. This, too, was one of the queen's weaknesses. The heaviest drinker was the Vicomte de Noailles. Lafayette was not very expert at any of these vices. Moreover, Adrienne's tastes did not permit much gaiety. He was a little envious, however, of young Noailles' accomplishments and tried to imitate them. On one occasion he drank more than he could carry, and had to be put in a carriage and sent home. All the way to the hôtel he kept mumbling, "Don't forget to tell the Vicomte de Noailles how much I drank."[6]

Lafayette's set soon began to talk of themselves as the Court Club. This name they retained as long as the principal scene of their activity was Versailles. But a fresh attraction took them elsewhere. The café, well known to three generations on the left bank of the Seine, was a relatively new institution on the right bank. Young people used to flock to the little village of the Porcherons, just outside the walls of Paris at the foot of Montmartre, where many of the most famous cafés were now to be found. Here was the Cabaret de l'Épée-de-Bois, which the Court Club began to visit frequently. Soon they came to speak of themselves as the Society of the Wooden Sword (*Société de l'Épée-de-Bois*). The new name won Lafayette's approbation as more republican, when, a few years later, he had begun to have less aristocratic notions.[7] Yet it had no political significance to him when it was actually adopted. For there was very little interest in politics among the members of the Society of the Wooden Sword. Around them young bourgeois gentle-

---

[6] *Correspondance entre le Comte de Mirabeau et le Comte de la Marck pendant les années 1789, 1790 et 1791*, ed. Ad. de Bacourt, I (Paris, 1851), 63–64.

[7] Lafayette to Mme Lafayette, June 19, 1777, *Mémoires*, I, 96, and n. 2.

men were also forming clubs, and earnestly discussing the newest radical literature—a play by Voltaire, an essay by Rousseau, the plates of Diderot's *Encyclopédie*, or a chapter of Raynal's provocative *History of the two Indies*. But the Society of the Wooden Sword preferred to discuss horses, whist, and quadrilles.

Once, however, Lafayette and his friends did nearly get into trouble on a political issue. It was for making fun of the Parlements, the highest law courts of the land. The Parlementarians had recently become great popular heroes. In a state where absolutism had developed to a point unknown elsewhere in Europe, with the possible exception of Turkey and Russia, the prestige of the thirteen Parlements and their traditional right to postpone the registration of the king's decrees had become almost the only effective barrier to the complete achievement of autocracy. During the last twenty-five years of Louis XV's reign the Parlements had on several occasions effectively questioned the right of the king to make laws of his own free will and to levy new taxes without any consideration other than his own needs. Their greatest success had come in 1764 when they had obliged the king to abolish the Jesuits, an organization which in France had resisted every effort toward freedom and had been among the chief supports of absolutism. Since that triumph, however, the Parlements had fought an uphill battle, and finally, in 1771, Louis XV had entirely set aside these courts and exiled their members.

Popular sympathy went with them. They were not really fighting for the cause of the people. These were nobles—nobles of the robe, to be sure, looked down upon by the nobles of the sword, but proud none the less, and including among their number some of the finest and most ancient of the gentility. They were only trying to re-establish the right of the aristocracy to share in the government of France, using their control of these principal law courts as a weapon in this effort. Yet, in the struggle against new decrees, new taxes, and Jesuits, they were fighting the common enemy—the absolutism of the Bourbons; and the people of the thirteen cities in which they held their respective sessions made no secret of their support of the Parlementarians. Louis XVI had hardly ascended his grandfather's throne when, in keeping with the rôle of enlightened monarch which he had chosen to play, he decided to re-establish the Parlements. The French populace rejoiced.

But the Society of the Wooden Sword cared little for Parlements and public opinion. These young noblemen and ladies, not much interested in current political problems and very conscious of their superiority to common people, looked upon the entire episode as somewhat of a joke, and made fun of the stern old Parlementarians. On several occasions they burlesqued the meetings of the Parlement of Paris. One of the king's brothers played the part of the presiding judge; others took the rôles of counselors, prosecutors, and lesser members of the court. In one of these performances Lafayette played the character of chief prosecuting attorney (*procureur-général*). The young iconoclasts enjoyed themselves immensely, until the king's ministers heard about it. Some of the older courtiers were shocked by such a public display of disrespect for the official nobility, and anxious to take advantage of any pretext to have the boisterous young blades sent away from court, induced Maurepas, the king's chief minister, to propose to Louis XVI that their indiscretion be appropriately chastised. Before Maurepas could get the king's ear, however, the young Comte de Ségur, one of Lafayette's best friends, learned of the minister's intention and took it upon himself to inform Louis beforehand about the insult to the parlementary dignitaries. His Majesty thought the episode very amusing, and when Maurepas tried to get the king's permission to break up the group of merrymakers by sending some of them away from the court, the gentle monarch advised doing nothing about it for the present. Louis admitted that far from being angry, he considered it good sport.[8]

The prestige of the Noailles family reached its highest point during this winter of 1775. The young Queen Marie Antoinette wanted one of her favorites, the Duc de Fitz-James, to become a marshal. But the new minister of war, the Duc de Muy, in-

[8] Ségur, I, 42-43.

sisted that there were other men (including himself) more deserving. To satisfy both his queen and his minister, Louis XVI created seven marshals, and among them were the Duc de Noailles and his brother, the Duc de Mouchy. Public opinion soon attached to each of the seven new marshals one of the seven cardinal sins—to the Duc de Noailles, pride, and to the Duc de Mouchy, avarice.[9] Yet, even though there were by this wholesale promotion sixteen marshals of France, it was unprecedented that two members of the same family should be so honored at the same time. In the last three generations of Noailles there now had been four marshals of France. The brilliance of his father-in-law's name opened to young Lafayette weighty doors that would otherwise have remained securely closed against him. At one of the queen's balls he had the great honor of being designated as her partner in a quadrille. He distinguished himself, however, only by his awkwardness. She laughed at him, and the courtiers around her were not at all loath to join in the merriment at his expense.[10]

Lafayette also went to the masquerade balls of the Opéra, less formal affairs which more respectable society did not attend unless carefully disguised under dominos and masks. The queen sometimes attended these, too; so did Mme du Barry, who had been exiled from court since Louis XV's death. On one occasion, when Lafayette went with a group including the queen, Marie Antoinette, taking his arm, asked him to engage in conversation with Mme du Barry, whose domino he knew. Lafayette did so, under the flattering impression that this was the first time the queen had ever seen Mme du Barry. As a matter of fact, the queen had spoken to the fallen favorite several times before, but the meeting which Lafayette arranged was perhaps the first under such informal circumstances—in a place where the queen herself should not have been.[11]

[9] Hardy, "Mes loisirs," p. 49, Bib. Nat., fonds français 6682 (under date of March 25, 1775); [Bachaumont], XXX, 216 (supplement to entry for March 31, 1775).

[10] Bacourt, I, 61–62.

[11] For Lafayette's version of this episode, see Sydney, Lady Morgan, *Passages from my autobiography* (London, 1859), pp. 94–95; and Cloquet, p. 270. For relations of Marie Antoinette and Mme du Barry, see A. Arneth and A. Geffroy, *Correspondance*

Despite a certain amount of this easy camaraderie between the queen and some of the members of the Society of the Wooden Sword, the comments of scandalmongers were unjustified. Some years later there were backstairs whispers about Lafayette and the queen.[12] They were groundless. The queen had no great regard for the pale, lanky, red-haired son-in-law of the Noailles, whose pointed nose and receding forehead made him look like a bird. Few of the people at court admired him. Indeed, the air of quiet reserve which he always maintained made some of his companions feel that he was constantly brooding over some deep dissimulation.[13] The marquis was conscious of this suspicion but explained his introspective nature to himself as the effect of secret pride, sensitiveness about his awkward manner, and a tendency to be observant.[14] He was not very happy at court, where it was more important to know how to sit a horse well and to dance gracefully than to turn a phrase neatly into Latin. Despite his best efforts to acquire the *bon air*, he was obliged to realize that he was not cut out for a courtier.

Just as Lafayette had decided that life at court was not for him, his wife's relations tried to find a permanent position for him there. The Marshal de Noailles almost secured him a post in the service of the Comte de Provence, the elder of the king's brothers. That was too much. It was a bit of patronage that Lafayette determined not to accept. It might make of him merely a noble retainer for the rest of his life and bring to an end the military career he so wistfully desired. To put a stop to their well-meaning efforts without openly defying his family, the young marquis deliberately picked a quarrel with the Comte de Provence. One day, at a masked ball, recognizing the prince under his disguise, Lafayette engaged him in conversation. Provence began to show off his good Bourbon memory, and Lafayette interrupted him to say that he need not go to so much

secrète entre Marie-Thérèse et Mercy-Argenteau, I (Paris, 1874), 161–62, 187, 218, 263–64, 366–67, 370–71, 401; cf. "Madame du Barry, souvenirs du Comte d'Espinchal" in *Revue retrospective*, VI (1887), 193 n.

[12] Lady Morgan, p.113.

[13] Bouillé, *Souvenirs et fragments*, I, 134.   [14] *Mémoires*, I, 7.

trouble to prove that memory served fools in the stead of minds. The prince was willing to overlook the insult, if he could be convinced that Lafayette had not known to whom he had addressed this rebuke. But a few days later, when the two men met again and the comte asked if Lafayette knew with whom he had talked at the masquerade, the incorrigible lad replied, "Yes, he who wore that mask now wears a green coat." There was nothing for the comte to do but to turn the back of that coat on the defiant youth, and the position in his service was never again offered.[15]

The boy might have considered this act a personal victory and derived some satisfaction out of it. It was, indeed, a sort of declaration of independence. But from the point of view of people who counted, it was a tactless blunder. Having deliberately closed behind him the doors to a courtier's career, the young Auvergnat now had no choice but to follow his family's tradition of military glory. When the time came for the regular army maneuvers at Metz in the summer of 1775, he welcomed the change of atmosphere which it afforded. Even here he soon learned that the glory of the Champetières was overshadowed by the prestige of the Noailles.

It was during this summer that young Lafayette became a full-fledged captain in the Noailles Dragoons. Amid the practice drills and marches around Metz, D'Ayen wrote to the minister of war reminding him that Lafayette's commission as captain was to be definitely conferred when he reached his eighteenth birthday, and pointing out that that event would soon take place. The minister did what was expected of him, and upon reaching the designated age, Lafayette took command of the company from which the Prince de Poix had gone to the colonelcy of the Noailles Dragoons.[16] The command of this regiment was the property of Adrienne's family. The marshals, the Duc d'Ayen, and the Prince de Poix had headed it in turn. One of the sons-in-law of the Duc d'Ayen would probably some day succeed the present commander. The Vicomte de Noailles

---

[15] Cloquet, p. 101; *Mémoires*, I, 8, and note; J. Q. Adams, *Oration on the life and character of Gilbert Motier de Lafayette* (Washington, 1835), p. 15; see also p. 158 below.

[16] D'Ayen to Muy, August 24, 1775, A.M.G., dossier 1261.

had the right name and other qualifications for the post, but as a younger brother of the Prince de Poix he was never likely to inherit enough money to buy the office, as his predecessors had done. Lafayette, therefore, was the most logical candidate whenever Poix should withdraw or seek a higher rank. If Gilbert remained patient, a successful military career seemed practically assured him.

The general in command of the army to which the Noailles Dragoons were attached was the notorious Comte de Broglie. This mysterious gentleman had played a leading part in the secret diplomacy of Louis XV's reign, distinguishing himself particularly by his intrigues in Poland. Just before the death of the old king the unsavory reputation of some of Broglie's schemes had deprived him of much of his influence. But now he was once more a powerful figure in French politics and was secretly in touch with the ministers of Louis XVI.

Broglie had long been considering the possibility of an invasion of England as a means of destroying the inveterate enemy of France. When, however, the English colonies in America began to quarrel with the mother-country, Broglie began to feel that the best way for France to avenge herself upon her more successful rival was to encourage and aid revolt in the new world. As the struggle developed into open and armed rebellion, Broglie decided that the colonies ought to have a skilled French officer as their *generalissimo*, and could think of no one better qualified for the post than himself. Who could tell but that eventually he might become head of the new American state—a sort of stadtholder of the thirteen colonies?

Broglie admitted a few of his most trusted companions into his scheme—especially two of his officers named Kalb and Mauroy. Johann Kalb, better known as Jean Dekalb, was a Bavarian of peasant origin who had turned up in France with the title of "baron," and had become a professional soldier. He had served with distinction in the French army during the War of the Austrian Succession, and again, under Broglie, during the Seven Years' War. After that conflict, upon the recommendation of Broglie and with the aid and consent of the French foreign office, he had investigated the possibilities of an invasion of England and also of a revolt in England's American colonies. Knowing how to speak English, he had gone to these colonies and had become familiar with the American political scene. This made him a useful man for Broglie's purposes. The Vicomte de Mauroy was also personally devoted to Broglie. Both men were cool and competent, and could be relied upon to give able assistance to an enterprise which, without harming others too much, was likely to benefit themselves greatly.

It was not until 1776 that Broglie's plans fully matured.[17] But even in 1775 he was anxious to promote the American cause in France and to inspire sympathy for the American colonies in the young officers under his command. It so happened that while the summer maneuvers of 1775 were taking place, the Duke of Gloucester came to visit Metz. Gloucester, brother of King George III of England, was known to be opposed to the policies of his government, both from political motives and for personal reasons, since the king disapproved of his marriage with Horace Walpole's illegitimate niece. Broglie invited Gloucester as guest of honor to a dinner at which were also present some of the more prominent of his junior officers. Lafayette was among them.

At the dinner table the conversation soon came around to the Americans, who had recently created a Continental Congress, resisted the English troops at Lexington and Concord, and named Washington commander-in-chief of the Continental Army. Gloucester spoke with admiration of the Americans' behavior and expressed sympathy for their cause. Lafayette said nothing, but he was greatly affected. He hated the English and he had a grudge to settle with them. He vaguely felt that the success of England would mean the final annihilation of France's already diminished empire, while the victory of the Americans would entail the destruction of England's overgrown dominion. His best wishes went out to the revolting colonies.[18]

[17] Arthur Lee to "Colden," February 13, 1776, Wharton, *Revolutionary diplomatic correspondence of the United States*, II, 74, and note.

[18] Jared Sparks (*Writings of George Washington*, V, 445), depending probably on an account put at his or Ducoudray-Holstein's disposal by Lafayette (see below p. 82), places the dinner with Gloucester in 1776, but Lafayette, in 1828, when he saw Sparks,

Upon his return to Paris and the court in the autumn of 1775, Lafayette once more joined the group of young men and women among the aristocracy whose chief purpose in life was to enjoy themselves as best they could. Adrienne seldom went with him in his searches for amusement. He was fond of her, to be sure, but she was a carefully brought-up young lady whose simplicity did not permit her to join in all the activities of her husband's circle. A large part of the year immediately following their marriage she had spent in a religious struggle that tormented her soul. Too sincere to submit in conventional fashion to a merely formal ceremony, Adrienne had postponed her first communion until her doubts should be removed. Only when she was fifteen years of age and had begun to expect her first child did conviction come. On the eve of her first wedding anniversary, Adrienne, feeling that she was in a state of grace, peacefully partook of the sacrament. Her baby was born on December 15, 1775. Adrienne had wanted it to be a boy. The Marshal de Noailles, her grandfather, had been greatly disappointed that his only son had had only daughters and hoped that his granddaughters might remedy this deficiency.[19] He was to be disappointed again. Adrienne's child was a daughter, to whom they gave several names, in the approved fashion, though she was generally known as Henriette. She turned out to be a sickly infant who required much of her mother's time and attention. The young wife was content to stay at home while her husband tried to find amusement elsewhere.

Lafayette moved in a circle where the men had been married while still in their teens to girls with whom they were even less acquainted than Lafayette had been with his bride. Most of them regarded marriage as a family duty which had nothing to do with love. They looked for love elsewhere. It was the fashion which had been set by the old king, and which the new one had

---

had himself begun to believe the legend that had grown up around his departure for America. Gloucester's visit to France was in 1775 (see Doniol, I, 98) and had therefore only a barely remote connection with Lafayette's decision a year later. Cf. Lafayette's *Mémoires*, I, 8–10, and note.

[19] Mme Lafayette to Lafayette, December 24, 1779, in Huntington Library, HM 9426.

not yet been able to change, that a young gentleman should have an illicit flame or two. Lafayette was no exception, but his luck with women was no better than with wine or with song. Only the Comte de Ségur knew about the younger man's disappointment. Everybody else would have been surprised to learn that the boy whom they thought cold and taciturn entertained so passionate an interest in a lady. But Ségur knew how deep was Lafayette's infatuation.

Ségur also was acquainted with his friend's inamorata. So were all the other young men who moved in the Duc de Chartres' circle at the Palais Royal. Here the dashing Vicomte de Noailles was one of the most welcome figures, and Lafayette tried to keep pace with him. The Comtesse de Hunolstein, one of the most beautiful ladies in Paris, wife of the colonel of the Chartres Cavalry Regiment, was frequently at these gatherings as lady-in-waiting to the Duchesse de Chartres. Lafayette fell pitifully in love with her, but she paid him very little attention. The Duc de Chartres was himself generally believed to be her favored lover, though Lafayette saw a rival in every other young man of his set. It was his good friend Ségur of whom he was especially jealous. One winter's night in 1776 the disappointed boy stayed until dawn in Ségur's room, arguing and cajoling, in an effort to persuade his friend to fight a duel for the love of the ungracious lady. Ségur insisted he was not at all interested in her and refused to fight.[20] Unhappy, indeed, was the lover who could not even pick a quarrel with one of his best friends for the heart of a lady who had already granted it to yet another.

There was too much of the ruggedness of his native Auvergne mountains in Lafayette's soul to make it possible for him to play adequately the part of a son-in-law of the Noailles. He could neither dance nor drink and was unfortunate in love. The Marshal de Noailles was particularly disappointed in him. He and various other members of the family even took the trouble to talk to Ségur about it. Wouldn't he use his influence with his younger friend to rouse him from his nonchalance, excite him into some kind of activity, put a little more vigor

[20] See Appen. II below.

into his character? Ségur knew that they were mistaken in believing Lafayette slow of spirit and unemotional, for he had not yet forgotten the sleepless night the disconsolate marquis had only recently made him spend. Still he could not tell the Marshal de Noailles about that. So he only smiled and kept his own counsel.[21]

As long as Lafayette remained an officer in the Noailles regiment with a good opportunity of one day becoming its colonel he could continue to feel some self-respect. To be sure, if he ever became the commander of the Dragoons, it would probably be only because of the influence of his wife's family and his own ability to buy commissions. But that was not uncommon among the young men of his class, though the proudest of them counted upon their fathers rather than their fathers-in-law for promotion. Even the chances of attaining distinction in the French army, however, were soon in large part taken away from Lafayette. A new minister of war, the Comte de St. Germain, was named at the end of 1775. As one who had been appointed to a ministry committed to a policy of reform, the new head of the war department soon began to wipe out some of the corps and to diminish the number of officers in others. Lafayette's old regiment of the Musketeers was entirely abolished. The Noailles Dragoons was one of those which were reorganized. Many of its officers were put in the reserve on part-pay—réformé, as the official French term had it. St. Germain, a veteran who had risen from the ranks, was particularly adverse to young captains who had seen no real military service and had been promoted only by family influence. These he placed in the reserve regardless of the indignation of their high and mighty families. Lafayette was just the kind of young, inexperienced captain to attract St. Germain's attention. Even the authority of the Noailles could not long save the young marquis from the relentless zeal of the new minister. On June 11, 1776, Lafayette ceased to be an active officer of the king.[22] He still re-

<hr>

[21] Ségur, I, 106–7.

[22] See Lafayette's several états de services in A.M.G., dossier 1261; on the original one, after "réformé 1776," another hand has added in pencil "11 juin." See also ibid., the bon of the king, dated March 3, 1779, where Lafayette is referred to as "capitaine

tained part of whatever emoluments and privileges went with his rank, but as a captain in reserve he could no longer look forward with the same assurance to a successful military career. Like many other young nobles hoping for advancement in the army, he could expect to find promotion hard to secure in a period of peace, retrenchment, and military reform.[23]

Lafayette had come to the point where if he surrendered to circumstances, as he had been content to do in the past, he would develop into nothing more than an unsuccessful and negligible hanger-on at court. He would shine dimly in the reflected glory of the Noailles, live more or less peacefully with Adrienne and his growing family, adore Mme de Hunolstein from a distance, and continue to feel self-conscious at the queen's balls among more poised and assured companions. Since he had quarreled with the Comte de Provence, a civil post would be difficult for him to obtain, and he would be obliged idly to await the time when he should be reinstated into active military service. It was not an engaging prospect.

But something else was brewing in his mind. His earliest recollections were of the tales of greatness he had learned at Chavaniac. His earliest ambition had been to roam the world in search of fame.[24] If only now the proper opportunity should present itself, they would all see the stuff of which he was made and would recognize how greatly they had misjudged him! His wealth and his person would be at the disposal of any venture that promised glory. Surely his enormous wealth at least ought to be good for something!

BIBLIOGRAPHY

Mercy-Argenteau was the ambassador of the Empress Maria Theresa at Versailles. One of his principal problems was the behavior of the empress' daughter, Marie Antoinette. The *Correspondance secrète entre Marie-Thérèse et Mercy-Argenteau*, ed. A. Arneth and A. Geffroy (3 vols.; Paris, 1874–75), is

réformé du Reg^t de Dragons de Noailles ... réformé en 1776." See also Appen. III below for other possible explanations of this *réforme* of Lafayette.

[23] Ségur, I, 101; *Correspondance secrète inédite sur Louis XVI, Marie Antoinette, la cour et la ville*, ed. M. de Lescure (2 vols.; Paris, 1886), I, 40; *Correspondance de Métra*, IV, 264.

[24] *Mémoires*, I, 7–8.

therefore a very full and exceptionally reliable source of information upon the activity of the queen's circle. On Lafayette's introduction of the queen to Mme du Barry the account followed here is that given by Sydney, Lady Morgan, in *Passages from my autobiography*, which is not exactly that given by Cloquet. Lady Morgan, who knew Lafayette intimately in the first years of the Restoration, set down his anecdotes soon after she heard him recite them, whereas Cloquet heard them much later and wrote them down only after a considerable interval. M. MacDermot Crawford, *The wife of Lafayette* (London, 1908), p. 45, argues that this meeting of the queen and Du Barry must have taken place before Lafayette's marriage, but, since Lafayette refers to Marie Antoinette as queen and not as dauphiness, this is scarcely possible.

The story of Lafayette's part in the last dinner of Mme du Barry and Louis XV is told here upon Cloquet's authority. This does not correspond with the account given by Henri Doniol, *Établissement des États-Unis d'Amérique*, I, 664 n., but Doniol does not indicate his source, and because of a definite pro-French bias and a frankly admitted propaganda purpose, his book must be used with caution. Nevertheless, because he knew the members of the Lafayette family (I, 652, n. 3) and was a zealous collector and editor of texts, his chapters on Lafayette are a veritable mine of information. Because it conforms to the known facts, Doniol's account of Lafayette's silence on the illness of Louis XV has been accepted here.

Edith Sichel, *The household of the Lafayettes* (London, 1910), pp. 60–61, narrates, in a fashion different from that followed above, the details of the quarrel between the Comte de Provence and Lafayette. Since she cites no sources, and since her book is full of errors and inventions, her interesting account of this episode has not been repeated here. The narration of this event by John Quincy Adams in the oration delivered before the joint session of Congress on December 31, 1834, and cited above, may have been derived from the letters of Cloquet in the *Evening Star*, but as they present the attitude of Lafayette in quite a different light, may also have been learned from conversation with Lafayette.

For other events here given Mme Lafayette's biography of the Duchesse d'Ayen in Lasteyrie, *Madame de Lafayette*, has been the principal source. This has been supplemented by the narratives of the Comte de Ségur (*Mémoires ou souvenirs et anecdotes* [3 vols.; Paris, 1825–27]), and of La Marck in A. de Bacourt's *Correspondance entre le Comte de Mirabeau et le Comte de La Marck* (3 vols.; Paris, 1851), I, 16–67. Ségur was a friend of Lafayette's during the period under discussion, and later (1777) married the Duchesse d'Ayen's much younger sister, thereby becoming Lafayette's uncle. La Marck was a friend of the Vicomte de Noailles and a frequent visitor at the hôtel of the Noailles. Ségur is friendly toward Lafayette; La Marck is unfriendly, having, at the time he wrote, become an apologist for Mirabeau, Lafayette's opponent in the first stages of the French Revolution. But La Marck's effort to be fair is shown by his admission that Lafayette was a more intelligent man than the Vicomte de Noailles (p. 64).

For other works used in the preparation of this chapter, see also Appendixes II and III below. On Kapp, *Johann Kalb*, see below pp. 81 and 149.

CHAPTER V

Absentee Landlord

IF ONLY young Gilbert de Lafayette had been of the more ancient branch of his family, he would have been at this point in his career a typical court noble of the Old Régime. In many other regards he conformed to type. He held the nobility of the robe and the bourgeoisie in contempt; he devoted his life to military pursuits—though none too strenuously; he occupied himself with the idle pleasures of the court circle. He differed from other courtiers merely because he had but recently come from a hopelessly provincial village and because his was but the third generation of the Champetières to hold the title of Lafayette and to have been received at court. It was these very disadvantages that distinguished him from his fellows, made him feel misfit and ill at ease, and caused him to be much more sensitive about his little reverses than they would have been. This keen consciousness of failure made him long more vehemently for a career which none of them could imitate.

If Lafayette could only determine upon what to do he had the means to do it. For he was rich—rich even for a great aristocrat. In that regard, indeed, he was far from typical of a large part of the court nobility, as many of them had small incomes or none at all, and were obliged to live upon such pensions and bounties as a munificent king awarded or to engage in various kinds of stock-jobbing and chicanery. His estates were large and profitable, and he was one of the small group of men at the court who could afford to live on their own revenues as absentee landlords.

For the beginning of this good fortune the marquis was indebted largely to his grandmother's careful management. Before

he was born and while he was still a child, she had devoted herself to the augmentation of his inheritance. In addition to the
improvement in his feudal relations which she had effected by
buying up the obligation of Chavaniac to its overlord and
acquiring other feudal rights in neighboring towns, she had
bought and sold woods and lands, and engaged in litigation to
secure her rights against the claims of neighboring nobles.[1]
Upon her death his estate as a Lafayette and a Champetière was
more compactly organized and more definitely secure than any
of his immediate male ancestors had had time or inclination to
make it; and to it, by the simple process of outliving closer
relatives, he had added the huge fortune of the Marquis de La
Rivière.

The Marquise de Lafayette's legal adviser in laying the
foundation of her grandson's wealth had been the honest,
conscientious, and thoroughly competent lawyer, Jean Gerard.
It was he who since the dowager's death had been actually responsible for the management of all of Lafayette's properties,
though Mlle du Motier had taken her place as the overseer of
the estate in Auvergne. Gerard kept Gilbert's aunt informed of
what was being done about her nephew's possessions there, and
she furnished him with such details as he had occasion to demand. He also had frequently to enter into communication
with the Comte de La Rivière, the Abbé de Murat, and, after
Lafayette's marriage, with the Duc d'Ayen to secure their consent to some of his decisions. The estates that Lafayette had inherited from his grandfather La Rivière, Gerard was obliged
to manage through agents. The Chevalier de la Villebeaud was
his agent in Brittany, and M. Rossignol in Touraine, where
some of the Marquis de La Rivière's bequests were located.

Gerard sometimes went to these provinces in order personally
to supervise the work of his stewards. M. Rossignol had especially to be watched, as he had a bad temper and was always
quarreling with the local authorities. At one time this had ne-

---

[1] Le Puy, Archives départmentales de la Haute Loire, E2 684, pièces 3 and 14;
Archives de la Préfecture de Clermont-Ferrand, unclassified document marked "E. Lafayette, Don Delpy, 1905"; University of Chicago Library, DC 146, f. L2 A 12.

cessitated Gerard's going to Touraine to make peace. Rossignol
promised to be more careful in the future, but almost immediately upon Gerard's departure broke his promise by in-
sulting the local bailiff. Gerard then demanded his resignation,
which Rossignol refused to give. It was necessary to send his successor, a royal notary named Olivier, who happened to be Rossignol's brother-in-law, before the troublesome steward actually
did resign. This affair was managed by Gerard with the advice
of the Comte de La Rivière, whose lands in Touraine had likewise been under Rossignol's management.[2]

Gerard had his own differences with government officials.
They were frequently over matters of taxation. It was usual
for noblemen of the Old Régime to use whatever influence they
could bring to bear upon the authorities in order to lower their
taxes. It made small difference to them that the sum to be collected annually from each province was generally fixed in advance and that therefore the less each noble contributed the
more the middle class had to pay. The point was, wherever
possible, to avoid paying taxes, and a good advocate, even
though of the middle class, considered it his business to assist
his clients in that endeavor. For that reason, in 1774 Gerard
made a strenuous effort to reduce Lafayette's capitation tax.
In origin the capitation was a head tax, but in France it was now
levied according to class, regardless of privilege, and the upper
classes generally paid more than the lower, especially when they
paid taxes in more than one province. Gerard discovered that
Lafayette's capitation tax for 1774 in the province of Auvergne
was higher than for the preceding year, despite the fact that
he had already paid a similar one in Versailles. Hoping to get
at least a partial exemption, he instructed Mlle du Motier to
postpone payment until he could bring the matter up before
the collector of the capitation at the court. Gerard spoke of the
matter also to the Duc d'Ayen, who consented to lay a memoir
on the subject before the controller-general of finances himself.
After six months' delay Gerard was obliged to write Mlle du

[2] Gerard to Mlle du Motier, January 31, February 23, 1774, University of Chicago
Library, DC 146, f. L2 A3, Vol. I.

Motier to pay the Auvergne capitation. The increasing desire of the nobility to avoid taxation was counterbalanced by the growing need of the government for money; the existing government, Gerard was informed, wished to base the capitation not so much on one's social station, as before, but upon one's income. The controller-general agreed that where the same man was taxed in two places, the intendant of the province in which he paid the lower tax might order a proportionate reduction on the other, but as that had already been done in this particular case, Gerard's request that Lafayette be excused entirely from his capitation in Auvergne was denied. "I am very sorry, Mademoiselle," Gerard wrote Lafayette's aunt, "but we must admit that your nephew is very likely to be taxed much more in the future than now. We have to be content with the present arrangement."[3]

The unfavorable decision of the government on this matter was in part counterbalanced by certain favors which Gerard secured for Lafayette. In January, 1774, he informed Mlle du Motier that the village of Aurac was thenceforth to be permitted to have two fairs a year. Aurac has ever since had these two fairs and in large part owes whatever prosperity it now has to Lafayette's enterprising lawyer.[4] Lafayette also had good luck in avoiding the payment of the *octroi* (entry tax) on cheeses and game sent to him in Paris from his several estates. Gerard was able to register him at the city gates as proprietor of these lands, and thus secure special consideration for the marquis' shipments.[5] The meticulous administrator allowed no advantage which Lafayette might claim as a member of a privileged class to go by default.

In the meantime, Lafayette kept acquiring new lands. Sometimes this was effected by successful litigation over disputed properties—a common practice among the landlords of his day—and sometimes by purchase. Gerard and the other guardians

---

[3] *Idem* to *idem*, January 31, February 23, and July 8, 1774, *ibid.*

[4] *Idem* to *idem*, January 31, 1774, *ibid.*; Mosnier, *Château Chavaniac*, p. 22.

[5] Gerard to Mlle du Motier, December 28, 1774, University of Chicago Library, *loc. cit.*

of Lafayette believed it a good investment to buy new lands, and tried to make several acquisitions, even borrowing the money for this purpose when necessary. A large portion of land adjacent to the ancestral manor of La Fayette was thus purchased at a cost of forty thousand livres.[6] At about the same time they borrowed a huge sum of money in order to make an investment in a good piece of Paris real estate—the hôtel de La Marck. For some of his property, new as well as old, Lafayette owed faith and homage to the Comte d'Artois, to whose appanage some of these Auvergne lands had recently been assigned. Upon the performance of the ceremony of rendering faith and homage, this prince demanded of each of his vassals certain payments which some of them considered too high. One of them had to pay 279 livres and a brother of the Abbé de Murat 200 livres. Some of the Auvergne seigniors determined to protest, and Gerard was very much in sympathy with them. Lafayette and Gerard decided to postpone the ceremony of faith and homage until they received more reasonable treatment.[7]

In all this, also, Lafayette acted a part typical of the nobility of the Old Régime. He defended his interests against the royal family from above and against his own dependents below. He increased his holdings wherever possible. This was easier for him than for many of his peers, as he was rich, while poverty obliged some of them to sell the land they owned. Through Gerard, Lafayette, also quite typically, collected as much as he could out of the rents and feudal payments due him. When, for example, the contracts of the peasants and farmers of Vissac and St. Romain were renewed in 1774, Mlle du Motier had a local lawyer propose a plan for their revision. Gerard felt, however, that this local *commissaire* charged too much and wrote Mlle du Motier that he would prepare another plan which would be "more profitable for the seignior in whose name we act." By this plan the *commissaire* was to be paid in a lump sum and not until all the contracts were completed. The pay-

[6] *Idem* to *idem*, July 1, August 18, and December 28, 1774, and November 25, 1775, *ibid.*

[7] *Idem* to *idem*, December 28, 1774, *ibid.*

ment per unit of rent which had at first been suggested might become very large, and Gerard preferred a more definite agreement.[8] The contracts thus were drawn up in the usual feudal fashion with the interests of the noble lord well protected.

Quite typically again, Lafayette's legal adviser also dug up some old claims that had been allowed to remain forgotten until recent years. The most important of these was for a piece of the forest called the Boisgrand which had been given to the Marshal de Lafayette in the fifteenth century. The papers establishing the marquis' equity were never located and his title was therefore never made good by his lawyers. Nevertheless they did not hesitate to add to Lafayette's assets the indemnity they considered due him on this claim.[9]

So widespread and various were Lafayette's estates that it took Gerard over a year to prepare the statement of Lafayette's wealth which he had planned to present upon the young man's marriage. The preparation of this report (*compte de tutelle*) required extensive correspondence with Mlle du Motier at Chavaniac, the Chevalier de Villebeaud for the estates in Brittany, and M. Olivier for Touraine. Bad roads, irregular posts, high rates, and the precautions necessary against accident and robbery rendered communication even with Chavaniac exceedingly difficult.[10] The accounts of Mlle du Motier requested by Gerard in February, 1774, were not received until the end of June, and then turned out to be unusable because they were confused and inaccurate. The accounts from Brittany were delivered by the Chevalier de Villebeaud in person—but not until August. Gerard worked assiduously upon them with the Abbé de Murat's help, but it was not until the next year that he finished

[8] *Idem* to *idem*, August 18, 1774, *ibid.;* cf. Le Puy, Archives départementales, E2 684, no. 2.

[9] *Idem* to *idem*, May 13 and November 25, 1775, University of Chicago Library, DC 146, f. L2 A3, Vol. I; "Compte rendu sur la fortune du Général Lafayette à différentes époques de sa vie," Bibliothèque Universitaire de Clermont-Ferrand, dossier "Lafayette" in Auvergne collection, MS 14; also quoted in G. Chinard, *Letters of Lafayette and Jefferson* (Baltimore, 1929), pp. 303-15; see also Archives Nationales, T 1640, no. 61.

[10] Cf. Gerard to Mlle du Motier, May 13, 1775, University of Chicago Library, DC 146, f. L2 A3, Vol. I. See also above, pp. 33-34.

his report and submittted it to Lafayette's various guardians for consideration. Mlle du Motier was highly dissatisfied with the statement concerning Auvergne, because she believed it exaggerated the value of her nephew's property there and she would be held responsible for a greater sum than was actually forthcoming. Gerard hastened to assure her that in drawing up accounts of guardianship for a minor who was getting married "it was the custom to overestimate rather than underestimate his fortune" and that no one would hold her responsible for a single sou beyond the actual income of the Auvergne estate. On the contrary, he said, everybody was impressed with the scrupulousness with which she took care of her nephew's interests.[11]

And it was indeed impressive. With such zealous servants as Gerard and his devoted aunt, Lafayette was better off than if he had managed his own estate. He never had to worry about where his money would come from, and he therefore never learned its real value. This was already one of the most charming things about him to his friends and his merchants. Between April, 1775, and May, 1779, Mme de Lafayette, who was more careful than her husband, spent alone at Le Normand et Compagnie, silk merchants in Paris, over 5,320 livres,[12] an average of about 1,330 livres a year, or about $1,600 at present values. Lafayette's annual income at this time was about 146,000 livres, or about $175,000 today. His usual yearly expenditure was about 96,000 livres. There were not very many boys in France still in their teens who could as easily afford to purchase fame as he.[13]

Lafayette's revenues came chiefly from the rents and dues on his land. The Brittany estate produced annually about 60,000 livres, Auvergne 15,000, and Touraine 13,000. The payment of

[11] *Idem* to *idem*, February 23, May 15, July 1, August 18, December 28, 1774, and November 25, 1775, University of Chicago Library, DC 146, f. L2 A3, Vol. I.

[12] Archives Nationales, T 333.

[13] "Compte rendu sur la fortune du Général Lafayette," *loc. cit.*, and Gerard's successor, Morizot, to Mlle du Motier, December 27, 1777, in University of Chicago Library, DC 146, f. L2 A3, Vol. I. The figures in the *compte rendu* are given in francs, which, however, were at that time equivalent to livres.

interest on Mme de Lafayette's dowry brought 9,000 livres, rent on the hôtel de La Marck brought 9,000 livres more, and various other properties left him by the Marquis de La Rivière netted 24,000 livres. Most of these possessions he had never seen and knew nothing about.

In addition to being a rich absentee landlord Lafayette was also, in a smaller way, a capitalist. He and the ancestors from whom he had inherited his fortune had lent out certain sums of money at interest, and his income from this source was 16,000 livres annually. The only great commercial operation in which Lafayette was thus concerned was the French East India Company, which by this time was moribund, its monopoly of the French trade in the east having been abolished and its assets being in the process of liquidation. The remainder of Lafayette's loans were personal ones to various relatives and friends. Some of them had been made by the Marquis de La Rivière to gentlemen of prominent noble families and several to clerical institutions. A few smaller sums had been loaned by the old Marquise de Lafayette, his grandmother. Many grants were also being made by the Comte de La Rivière in Lafayette's name from his ward's funds. These loans were generally at 5 per cent, carefully specified in notes registered before Trutat, the notary nearly always employed by the La Rivières and Lafayette. These were most often perpetual loans, though on some of them a reduction of principal did occasionally take place.[14] Lafayette himself appears not to have made any loans at interest until later.

Thus without his having to do very much about it, Lafayette's fortune grew. Murat, Mlle du Motier, the Comte de La Rivière, the Comte de Lusignem, and principally Gerard did the investing and buying, while Mlle du Motier, Villebeaud, and Olivier did the actual superintending of the estates. Lafayette himself never seemed to give a thought to the question of whether the peasants on his several properties were better or worse off because of their lord's absence. He remembered only with fondness the respect that the people of Chavaniac had

[14] See n. 13 above, and Archives Nationales, T 1640, no. 61.

shown him when he was a child. Some years later, after the French Revolution abolished, nominally at least, the most trying of feudal abuses, he spoke of Chavaniac as a place of "nauseous distinctions" where he had been "a witness to the arbitrary and squeezing forms of our late government under which my neighbors, who, thank God, are no longer my vassals, did groan."[15] But that was in 1791. In the 1770's he knew very little about his neighbors' difficulties. As late as 1779 (after he had begun to be an enthusiast for liberty and equality), he did not even know whether any of them were still serfs, bound to the soil, and, when he wished to find out, had to inquire about it from his legal adviser, who himself had to ask Mlle du Motier.[16]

That his vassals might be groaning under the "arbitrary and squeezing forms" of the government was of little import to a young lord who had never visited his lands in Touraine and Brittany and went only rarely to his native rocks in Auvergne. Like those of most of his peers, his stewards were chiefly concerned with making as much money as possible, by the most profitable leases and contracts that could be arranged, out of the purchase, sale, rent, and exploitation of his property. The management of his estate was a hard-headed business matter, conducted in his name at least, even if he was himself perhaps not aware of what was going on. All over France there was taking place a similar "feudal reaction." Agents of the richer nobles everywhere searched among their dusty parchments for ancient and forgotten claims, renewed their contracts with their peasants in order to secure more favorable conditions, bought up good lands, lent out their surplus capital, and paid as little of their taxes as the authorities would permit. The nobility themselves were content for the most part to leave their estates to the management of professional supervisors while they amused themselves at Versailles, largely indifferent to the grow-

[15] Lafayette to "My dear friend," December 10, 1791, in Clements Library, Ann Arbor, Mich.; some of Lafayette's Gallicisms have been corrected in the quotation.

[16] Morizot to Mlle du Motier, September 4, 1779, in University of Chicago Library, DC 146, f. L2 A3, Vol. I.

ing demand for reform. In this regard Lafayette was altogether representative of the aristocrats of the Old Régime. If he was dissatisfied with his present lot, it was not because he had a superior sense of justice and a greater respect for the right. It was certainly not because he had passed under the insidious influence of Voltaire and the *philosophes*. It was because he felt self-conscious, inferior, and unhappy in a milieu for which his ancestry, early training, and awkward manner had not prepared him—because he was nothing more than a country squire among princes, dukes, and marshals, even though richer than most of them.

BIBLIOGRAPHY

In 1810 Lafayette made an appeal to Thomas Jefferson for some sort of compensation for his expenditures in the American Revolution. For this purpose he had his lawyer draw up a long account of the state of his finances at various periods of his life. Several copies of this were made and sent to Jefferson. One is reproduced in Gilbert Chinard, *The letters of Lafayette and Jefferson* (Baltimore, 1929), pp. 303–15. Another, which, in the spelling of proper names, has been followed here, is to be found in the Bibliothèque Universitaire de Clermont-Ferrand as indicated in the footnotes above. In the T series of the Archives Nationales are to be found the papers confiscated from the émigrés during the French Revolution. Lafayette's papers are contained in T 333 and T 1640. Unfortunately these are for the most part the records of his papers rather than the papers themselves. The pertinent materials in the departmental archives at Clermont-Ferrand and Le Puy are very few and not very helpful.

CHAPTER VI

The Broglie Intrigue

WHILE the disconsolate Lafayette was becoming more and more unhappy about the way in which his life was being arranged at home, elsewhere events were occurring that were soon to buoy up his hopes. Over three thousand miles away there was taking place the revolution in which he had been mildly interested since his meeting with the Duke of Gloucester. In the intervening months the revolting colonies in America had developed a distinct national spirit, had begun to think seriously of independence, and had established diplomatic relations with foreign powers. In 1776 they sent to France a commercial and political agent named Silas Deane, who was to try to win French popular and governmental support for his country.

Silas Deane's position in Paris was not an enviable one. He was ostensibly only a merchant, but everyone knew that if he found it possible, he was to take care of any diplomatic negotiation that might in any way aid the American rebels. When he arrived, the colonies had not yet declared their independence, and the attitude of the French government toward them was therefore undecided. Obviously a foreign nation would be exposing itself unnecessarily to British wrath if it interfered in an English domestic quarrel which neither of the contending parties had yet called a revolt. When finally the American colonies concluded that they could more easily secure the aid of England's enemies by declaring themselves a nation, it was not until October, 1776, three months after the Declaration of Independence, that Deane first heard of it, and then only unofficially. Since he had no definite instructions regarding the change in his own status which was effected by the new position of the revolted colonies and since he was occupied meanwhile with certain secret enterprises in the interest of his government, he waited until he received formal notice (November 7) to tell the Comte de Vergennes, Louis XVI's foreign minister, of his country's claim to a place in the family of nations. The French government was now free to adopt a less equivocal course toward the self-styled independent states.

The French government, however, was not of a single mind on this issue. All persons of importance at Versailles were agreed upon the desirability of splitting the British Empire. Yet some, like the king, were opposed to encouraging rebellion, even in a rival state, and therefore wished to keep out of the American affair. Others, like Maurepas, the prime minister, while favoring the revolt, were inclined to be cautious and were unwilling to risk entangling France too definitely until it was clear that France's allies, Spain and Austria, would be ready to aid her, at least morally, in case of armed conflict.

Of the entire government, Vergennes, the astute minister of foreign affairs, was the most active in behalf of the thirteen new states. He had spent most of his life as a diplomatic agent of his government in the effort to restore French prestige, so greatly dimmed by the defeats of Louis XV. Now, as chief at the foreign office, he was anxious, if he could, to carry on that policy by bringing about a corresponding diminution of British power. The revolt of England's finest colonies offered an opportunity which he could not allow to slip through his fingers unused. Nevertheless, since both public and official opinion in France was far from unanimous in favor of the American merchant-class rebels, he dared not be too openly on their side. Even now that they claimed the status of an independent nation and refused to be considered rebels any longer, he had to proceed discreetly. There was a very learned and competent English ambassador at Versailles, Lord Stormont, whose own cynicism with regard to French duplicity and whose excellent system of espionage made him suspicious of every move that Vergennes made. If the French foreign minister were not careful, he might get himself involved too deeply and be pitilessly exposed by Stormont before he was himself ready and before his colleagues were willing to play his game. Quite obviously it was Vergennes' rôle to wait until France's allies were prepared to support her in a war upon England and until the new United States of America should show by reasonable success in battle and by a certain amount of political firmness their ability to maintain themselves as a united and self-respecting group before he committed France to a war on their behalf. In the meantime, lest the rebellion die of inanition, he must, with as innocent an air as possible, allow it to be fed.

Even before the American Declaration of Independence, therefore, Vergennes had followed the policy, already known to his predecessors, of pretending to be perfectly neutral while actually winking at and even encouraging adventurers who hoped to make money or reputation out of the struggle between the American colonies and their mother-country.[1] One of these adventurers was the Comte de Broglie. Few ever guessed to what an extent Vergennes suspected the ulterior motives behind Broglie's sympathy with the Americans. There was, besides, no reason why Vergennes should pry too deeply into them. To him it was sufficient that Broglie wished to weaken England by the rupture of the British Empire. Yet open collaboration with the mysterious count would be too compromising, and so the minister carefully avoided having any official associations with the would-be stadtholder. Still, in some circles it was frankly suspected that Broglie had government support. Broglie's nephew and aide-de-camp, Théodore de Lameth,[2] thought so; so did Lord Stormont, the English ambassador in Paris.[3] Moreover, Dekalb, Broglie's devoted friend and fol-

---

[1] For the policy of France, see Doniol, II, 50–62; and letters of Deane to the Committee of Secret Correspondence in October–November, 1776, Wharton, *Revolutionary diplomatic correspondence of the United States*, II, 167–68, 173–75, 183–84, 190–92, and 195–200. See also C. F. Adams (ed.), *Works of John Adams*, III, 389.

[2] Lameth, p. 106.

[3] Stormont to Weymouth, Paris, February 5, 1777, Public Record Office, State Papers, France 78/301, no. 21; April 9, 1777, *ibid.*, S.P. 78/302, no. 62; April 16, 1777, *ibid.*, no. 69; May 7, 1777, *ibid.*, no. 82; and Wharton, I, 395.

lower, was definitely in collusion with the department of war.[4]

Broglie kept steadily in touch with the American agent in Paris. The commercial needs of the colonies were taken care of by Deane through merchants, feigned or real, of greater or less standing and reputation, with and without the approval of the French government. But the American representative felt that in addition to ammunition and equipment, the newborn army needed trained officers. The idea of sending European soldiers of distinguished reputation to America originated with Arthur Lee, an American patriot in London, who had been the first to propose the Comte de Broglie as commander of the American army. On Lee's advice the recruitment of experienced military men in France was suggested to Deane by Beaumarchais, dramatist and adventurer, now secretly engaged in harming England by befriending America.[5] Already actively occupied in sending guns, uniforms, and money to the revolting colonies, the resourceful littérateur also undertook to deal with some French officers who, for a variety of reasons, wished to go to America. In order the better to attract such people Deane promised them good pay and high rank. The long peace and the difficulty of securing promotion in the French army caused his generosity to seem particularly persuasive to many discouraged careerists in France.

Some of the leading personages in Paris volunteered their services to help Deane make the acquaintance of these men. The Comte de Broglie was especially helpful. He gave frequent parties at his home, where young nobles attended and where the

---

[4] Dekalb to St. Paul, chef des bureaux de la guerre, November 7, 1777, *American historical review*, XV (1910), 562–67; cf. Doniol, I, 639–40, and Kapp, pp. 79–81. Lafayette, some years later, stated that Dekalb's subsequent departure for America "was encouraged by the Comte de Broglie and secretly approved by the French government"; see below, p. 146. Among the items of expense for which DeKalb asked to be reimbursed by Congress in 1777 was the cost of his "several goings to and comings from the King's residences on account of my going to serve in America"; see Elizabeth S. Kite, "Lafayette and his companions on the 'Victoire' (Part II)," *Records of the American Catholic Historical Society*, XLV (1934), 165.

[5] Lee to "Colden," February 3, 1776, Wharton, II, 74; Beaumarchais to Deane, July 26, 1776, *Deane papers*, I (New York, 1887), 163.

American war was the favorite subject of conversation. At these parties the Vicomte de Noailles was, as always, one of the lions, and Lafayette frequently came with him.[6] Soon young aristocrats of proved military experience came to see Deane and to offer their aid. By the end of 1776 Deane was "well-nigh harassed to death with applications of officers to go to America."[7] Before long he was ready to send off two boatloads of Frenchmen to serve the American cause.

The self-styled "Baron" Dekalb was one of the first officers in whom Silas Deane became interested. On November 4 Dekalb secured a leave of absence from the minister of war allegedly "in order to leave the kingdom for two years to attend to his affairs." Broglie almost immediately took him to see Deane. Two interviews between the three men took place on November 5, 1776.[8] Deane at the time had no instructions to recruit French officers for the American troops. Nevertheless he had become convinced that the presence of some influential French soldiers in the American ranks would not only improve the Continental Army but would also increase the interest of the French government in its success. Dekalb easily impressed Deane, besides, with his ability and his ostensible love of liberty. Hence, though with some misgivings, the American agent decided to enrol the "baron." Negotiation between Deane and Dekalb resulted in a definite contract on November 7. Dekalb, who had only the rank of lieutenant-colonel in the French army, though with the privileges of brigadier in the colonies, was to become a major-general in the American forces and to receive 12,000 livres besides. In the same contract Lieutenant Duboismartin, brother of the Comte de Broglie's secretary, was appointed the new general's aide-de-camp with the rank of major. Dekalb's contract stated very frankly that he had been induced "to serve the cause of liberty in America" on

[6] Lameth, pp. 105–6; cf. Count Mathieu Dumas, *Memoirs of his own time* (Philadelphia, 1839), p. 15, on the activity of the Marquis de Castries in this regard.

[7] Deane to the Committee of Secret Correspondence, November 28, 1776, Wharton, II, 98.

[8] St. Germain to Dekalb, November 4, 1776, Kapp, p. 296; Dean to the Committee of Secret Correspondence, November 6, 1776, Wharton, II, 191.

the advice of "some generals of the highest reputation and several other noblemen of the first rank."[9]

The news of this arrangement soon became common property and several ambitious or dissatisfied officers began to address themselves to Dekalb in the hope that they might be permitted to accompany him on his quest for high rank and livres in America. Dekalb introduced some of them to Deane, and they all had good reason to be convinced of American generosity. Deane seldom promised less than a captaincy. Many of those thus recommended for service in the American army were soldier-adventurers, close friends of the Comte de Broglie. Mauroy was appointed major-general on November 20. Several others who had seen service under Broglie and were friendly toward his project were also included on Deane's list. By December 1 Deane had drawn up a roll of sixteen officers who were to leave for America under Dekalb's orders. The success of the Broglie scheme seemed assured.

All around Lafayette, and particularly at the Comte de Broglie's parties, many young noblemen talked eagerly about their desire to go to America. The Vicomte de Noailles was the most enthusiastic of them, and the faithful Lafayette, anxiously seeking a means of escape from frustration and discontent, found it easier than usual to share his brother-in-law's feelings in this regard. Broglie was not particularly anxious, however, that Lafayette should become one of his emissaries. The count had fought in the war in Italy, where Lafayette's uncle had died, and he had been present when Lafayette's father had perished at the Battle of Minden. He had therefore no desire to see the last of the Lafayettes go off on a venture from which he might never return and about which the young man's family might in any case feel resentful. So he tried to dampen the marquis' ardor. "I will not be accessory to the ruin of the only remaining branch of your family," he told Lafayette.[10] But Lafayette refused to be discouraged, and the support of his

---

[9] Contract quoted at length by G. A. Boutwell, "Silas Deane and the coming of Lafayette," in *New England magazine*, VIII, N.S. (1893), 170; *Deane papers*, I, 343–45.

[10] Sparks, *Writings of George Washington*, V, 446; cf. Lafayette, *Mémoires*, I, 11.

more self-assertive brother-in-law gave him greater confidence of ultimate success.

Noailles and Lafayette soon discovered that their good friend, the Comte de Ségur, likewise looked hopefully across the Atlantic for glory and promotion. Ségur had spent the summer at Spa, in the Bishopric of Liége, where gentlemen of all nations came to take the water and to air their views. The favorite subject of conversation among them had been the American revolt, and everyone was on the side of the insurgents. Ségur, loyal French nobleman that he was, had found it easy to feel sympathy for those who were fighting the English. When, upon his return to Paris, he learned that the American agent in France was appointing French officers to the American army at ranks correspondingly higher than their status in the French service, he became more than ever anxious to offer his sword to the rebel cause.[11]

The three young men talked it over among themselves and determined upon a course of action. Until they should make their arrangements with Deane, receive the consent of their government, and gather the necessary means together, they decided to keep their plans a secret. The soldiers who had thus far offered to go to America were men who had no standing in society. The government could afford to adopt an attitude of indifference or injured innocence with regard to what they did. The volunteering of several noblemen attached to the court, however, would rouse great interest in all quarters, would appear too patent a violation of France's neutrality, and might easily lead to official opposition. While they could count upon the secret good wishes of most of the government, they realized that public policy would demand that the ministers act openly as if displeased and, if it became necessary to do so for the sake of appearances, punish them. Accordingly, Noailles, Ségur, and Lafayette agreed that they must proceed with the utmost caution.[12]

[11] Ségur, I, 74–75 and 99–105; Lameth, pp. 105–6.

[12] For the frequently alleged interview of these three friends with Silas Deane in August, 1776, see below, Appen. V.

Since all three lads were minors, discretion required that they should take no decisive steps without the consent of their parents or guardians, as well as the proper military authorities. The Vicomte de Noailles thought that the entire matter could satisfactorily be left to him. He wrote to the ministers for permission to go to America,[13] and tried to get the Duc d'Ayen to second him, with the expectation that if he were allowed to go, his two friends would be also. The vicomte spoke to the duke about it several times, but without success. One day, in the presence of Lafayette, young Noailles again put the matter before their father-in-law. He would like the Duc d'Ayen, the vicomte said, to use his influence with Maurepas to let him enlist in the American cause. D'Ayen again appeared to hesitate. Lafayette broke in to say that he would like to fight in America, too. That was too much for D'Ayen. "I'll make no such request for you," he shouted at Lafayette. The boy was deeply hurt. To be thus humiliated before his friend and brother-in-law whom he so much admired determined the marquis all the more to persevere in his plans.[14]

In desperation the disappointed lad went again to see his former commander, the Comte de Broglie, the only man among his older acquaintances who seemed to be well disposed toward him. When Broglie learned what had happened, he became more interested than ever before in the marquis' plight. A resentful youth with plenty of money, important connections, and very little knowledge of the ways of the world might prove very useful. Since the whole matter had to be handled most secretly anyway, D'Ayen and the rest need never know the older man's part in influencing young Lafayette's behavior. Broglie, besides, could truthfully say that he had tried to dissuade the lad, and that it was not his fault if the last of the Lafayettes, unwilling to stay at home with "papa" and "mama," Adrienne, and his growing family, and play a backward rôle in court society,

[13] Noailles to the Comte de [Maurepas ?], [end of 1776], B. F. Stevens, *Facsimiles of manuscripts in European archives relating to America, 1773–1783*, VI (London, 1890), no. 608.

[14] Bacourt, I, 65–67; cf. Lameth, pp. 106–7.

persisted in his quest for glory. Broglie, therefore, now assumed an air of friendly co-operation. "Good," he exclaimed to the dis-heartened boy. "Get even! Be the first to go to America! I shall take care of it!"[15] And he sent the lad to make the ac-quaintance of his crony Dekalb.

The "baron" had just signed his contract with Deane and was now engaged in finding young officers to leave with him for Amer-ica. Early in November the Vicomte de Noailles, still hoping for the consent of the ministers, and the Marquis de Lafayette, still feeling that his father-in-law might relent and permit him to go with his brother-in-law, came to see the newly appointed general.[16] The Comte de Ségur was not with them, for he had already given up the plan. Finding that his family objected vehemently to the foolhardy notion of the young man and fear-ing that the ministry would not consent to the departure of such distinguished volunteers, the count had already reluctantly withdrawn from the scheme.[17] Noailles and Lafayette gave De-kalb to understand that the Duc d'Ayen would favor their en-listment in the insurgent cause on condition that they be given the rank of general officers. They told him how pleased they would be to serve with him in America and asked that he pre-sent them to Silas Deane. Dekalb promised to do so. Within a few days the Vicomte de Noailles decided he could not afford to cross his father-in-law and wrote to say that he had aban-doned the project. Lafayette, however, returned several times to see Dekalb, and Dekalb also went to see him. They met al-most every day in November. As Dekalb was readily admitted at the Noailles hôtel, even when Mme de Lafayette was with her husband, he never suspected that the young man was antici-pating the truth when he claimed that he had the consent of the Duc d'Ayen. On the contrary, Dekalb even believed that Mme de Lafayette knew what it was they so eagerly debated.[18]

Finally Dekalb introduced Lafayette to Deane, and on De-

[15] Lameth, p. 107; cf. Bacourt, p. 66.

[16] Dekalb to St. Paul, November 7, 1777, *loc. cit.*, p. 564.

[17] Ségur, I, 105-6.

[18] Dekalb to St. Paul, November 7, 1777, *loc. cit.*, p.564.

cember 7 the triumphant marquis signed his contract with the American agent. Dekalb wrote it out at their dictation. Lafayette insisted upon a major-generalship in the American army. Deane had given this high office to Dekalb, who was a gentleman fifty-five years of age and an experienced soldier, and to Mauroy, similarly an officer of mature years and long service in the French army, yet he hesitated to do so in the case of a lad who but recently had celebrated his nineteenth birthday, had never been under fire, and had held a captaincy only because of his father-in-law's influence. Lafayette pointed out, on the other hand, that he could expect to get his family's consent only if he were given a general's rank in the American army. Fully recognizing also that his youth and inexperience did not recommend him to Deane, the despondent volunteer argued that his position in society would be of some value to the American cause. His departure for the rebel camp was bound to create a "slight sensation" within important circles.

Since Lafayette asked for no remuneration, the young man's predicament was much easier for Deane to solve than Dekalb's or Mauroy's. The boy certainly appeared to be a different sort from the rest of the soldiers with whom the American agent had hitherto had to deal. The question of service in America was not a matter of livres and sous to him; he seemed anxious for no reward except rank and glory. He was the only one among them who had anything but his comfort to sacrifice, for, as far as Deane could tell, he was giving up a place in society which only a son-in-law of the Noailles with a fortune of his own could hold. The departure of such a volunteer would certainly stir up favorable excitement.

Deane decided to grant the boy his wish. The contract that they dictated to Dekalb explained very clearly the reasons for this unusual generosity. In addition to the feeling that the marquis' family would not agree to his crossing the sea to serve in a foreign country unless he were made a general, Deane, all too easily impressed, pointed to Lafayette's "high birth, his alliances, the great dignities which his family hold at this court, his considerable estates in this realm, his personal merit, his reputation, his disinterestedness, and, above all, his zeal for the liberty of our provinces" as good reasons in themselves for making Lafayette a general.[19] Major-General-Elect Lafayette now thought there would be no further difficulty; his family would consent, and all would go well. Nevertheless he expressly reserved to himself in a postscript to the contract "the liberty of returning to Europe when my family or my king shall recall me."

At the moment that Deane signed this agreement with Lafayette, the American agent was no longer ignorant of what Dekalb's guiding motive was in raising a contingent to go to America. Dekalb had already made it so clear that on December 6 Deane wrote to his government that they ought to take under consideration the advisability of naming the Comte de Broglie to take command of the American army.[20] But if Deane, who dictated the contract, and Dekalb, who had held the pen, knew why Broglie had begun to interest himself in young Lafayette's American aspirations, the fledgling major-general had no suspicions on that score. He saw around him only kindly and disinterested older friends. It was, besides, of small concern to him whether Washington or Broglie commanded the American army. Still if anyone had troubled to ask him, he would most probably have given his preference for his friend and former commander, arguing, like Dekalb, that such a leader would lend to the American cause not only good military knowledge but also much-needed prestige.

The only question that the young general now had to face was how to inform his family of his new distinction. The women could easily be overlooked. If Adrienne ever guessed what was going on, she never let anyone suspect that she knew.[21] Perhaps

[19] Facsimile of Deane's copy of the contract (in French) in Boutwell, *loc. cit.*, p. 172. Cf. Wharton, II, 220–21; the list of officers here given, however, was not drawn up until a later date. See below, Appen. V. Cf. also Deane to Robert Morris, May 26, 1777, Library of Congress, papers of the Continental Congress, Acquisition 2827.

[20] Deane to the Committee of Secret Correspondence, December 6, 1776, Wharton, II, 218.

[21] For discussion of whether or not Mme Lafayette knew of Lafayette's departure, see below, Appen. IV.

her mother, too, was aware of the conspiracy and did not object. But "papa" was the real enemy. He had so little confidence in Gilbert that not even a major-general's commission at the age of nineteen would impress him greatly. With the Vicomte de Noailles it was different. There was a young man whom one could trust on a hazardous project! The Duc d'Ayen finally had yielded to Noailles' entreaties and had asked Maurepas' permission for the elder of his two venturesome sons-in-law to go to America. It was even rumored that he was considering going to America himself.[22]

The formal petition to the minister was a mistake in tactics, however. For Maurepas, who had said and done nothing to prevent other young men from going to America, since they had not asked his permission, could not now officially give his approval to an act which would certainly be regarded by all English sympathizers as a hostile one. Broglie's friends even saw a certain advantage in rejecting D'Ayen's petition. To give the government's consent to D'Ayen's request on behalf of the Vicomte de Noailles would be to present Lord Stormont with good cause for complaint. To oppose the request openly would be to make Lord Stormont feel somewhat more reassured concerning French neutrality and keep him quiet long enough for the rest of Dekalb's troop to leave without protest. So when Maurepas did refuse to give Noailles permission to embark, they were not greatly disappointed. Duboismartin, Broglie's secretary, wrote Dekalb that he considered Maurepas's decision "exactly what it should have been, when a matter calculated for oral communication only is committed to writing."[23]

It was on the very day of Lafayette's triumphant agreement with Deane that he learned of his comrade's failure to secure the minister's approval. Without formal permission young Noailles would not go. There was no good reason why he should. Unlike Lafayette, he was still a successful soldier and social light. If

---

[22] Duboismartin [Broglie's secretary] to Dekalb, December 8 and 14, 1776, Kapp, pp. 90–91; Dr. Bancroft to Paul Wentworth [English spy], [May 27, 1777], in Stevens, III, no. 254; Dekalb to Mme Dekalb, April 6, 1777, Kapp, p. 106.

[23] Duboismartin to Dekalb, December 8, 1777, Kapp, p. 90.

the adventure could not be undertaken with the approval of the proper persons, he had no serious objections to dropping it. But to Lafayette, his brother-in-law's decision was a new and distressing blow, inflicted at the very moment of success. He had persistently hoped that Noailles would finally manage to join Dekalb and that the Duc d'Ayen, on finding that the younger of the two men had already made so impressive an agreement with Silas Deane, would consent to the departure of both. Now that D'Ayen had failed to get the sanction of the prime minister for Noailles, he would certainly refuse to let the viscount go and it would be futile to ask him to agree that the marquis venture forth alone.

Lafayette was in despair. Dekalb was to go off to Le Havre to take ship for America the next day. The men who he and Deane had agreed should accompany him were to join him there and sail as soon as possible. At the same time another group of French officers were expected to depart for America under General du Coudray. Some of these young soldiers noisily made the rounds of the Paris cafés, boasting of what a thrashing they were going to give the English. Lafayette had expected to be one of those to accompany Dekalb. But here it was the day before the scheduled departure from Paris and he was more certain than ever that his father-in-law would not allow him to leave. It looked again as if he would fail in this—the greatest undertaking of his life—just as he had failed in so many things already.

Once more Gilbert turned to Broglie. The old general, the friend of his father and his uncle, was now almost his only confidant, the only man, who, besides Dekalb, had aided him in his effort to justify himself in the eyes of the world. But Broglie unfortunately was out of town, having left for his country-seat at Ruffec. Early in the morning of December 8, Lafayette called instead upon the general's secretary, Duboismartin. Duboismartin was really not seriously perturbed about the marquis' predicament. Though the boy interested him a little and he wished to keep him on friendly terms with Broglie, he was very busy arranging for older men to join Dekalb and sending out information and instructions. Nevertheless Lafayette was visibly agitated and Duboismartin was kind enough to listen. After a long interview Lafayette went off to see Dekalb, but there was little encouragement that the old soldier could give him. As he said goodbye to the baron, Lafayette defiantly cried, "Till we meet again in America!"[24]

That evening the assiduous lad returned to Duboismartin's quarters. He took up at least three hours of the busy secretary's time in his two visits that day, lamenting his situation and mulling over possible courses of action. Finally the marquis decided to consult the Comte de Broglie. He wrote a letter asking for "advice and instructions," and begged Duboismartin to send it to Ruffec for him. He had deliberately chosen to have it go by post, so as to have more time for reflection before he received an answer. Duboismartin, however, felt that Lafayette would not leave for America. The Vicomte de Noailles, he thought, seconded by the rest of the impatient lad's family, would succeed in dissuading him.[25]

Before Broglie could send to the tormented Lafayette any counsel regarding a further course of action, Dekalb and his troop were back in Paris. The group that was to have sailed with him had made the big mistake of assuming that the French government did not care even to pose as preserving her neutrality. But news of the defeat of Washington at Long Island the preceding August had just been published in France and the friends of America were dejected. The French ministry now recognized a greater need for caution than before. Stormont made such vigorous complaints about the number of French soldiers who were openly departing for America that the ministry felt called upon at least to keep up appearances of friendliness toward the English. Orders were issued to the lieutenant-general of police to arrest "with plenty of publicity and severity" any French soldiers who openly declared that the government had ordered them to America,[26] so that the public might

---

[24] Dekalb to St. Paul, November 7, 1777, *loc. cit.*, p. 564.

[25] Duboismartin to Dekalb, December 8 and 14, 1777, Kapp, pp. 89–91.

[26] [Vergennes ?] to Lenoir, lieutenant-general of police, Versailles, December 10, 1776, Archives du Ministère des Affaires Étrangères, Correspondance politique, États-Unis

be assured that there was nothing official about their expedition. At the same time the port authorities at Le Havre were instructed to prevent the American volunteers from sailing.

Dekalb waited for a few days in the hope that he might yet receive permission to go, but soon Duboismartin requested him to return to Paris. The illustrious Benjamin Franklin had come to join Deane as agent for America and was daily expected in the capital. Deane had begun to hesitate about the entire matter. Papers that he had intended sending by the Vicomte de Mauroy he now delayed. Unless someone who spoke English well interested Franklin in the Comte de Broglie, Duboismartin feared that "some other party may approach this member of Congress with the same views as those we advocate." "If you cannot get away," Duboismartin went on, "I would like you to write to Mr. Deane, asking him whether or not the arrival of Mr. Franklin will effect any alteration in the form or spirit of his dispatches, or in the plans you have submitted to him for the choice of a commander-in-chief."[27] Dekalb accordingly wrote a long letter to Deane asking him to submit it to Mr. Franklin,[28] and shortly afterward returned to Paris.

Thus, as the year 1776 came to a close, it looked as if Broglie's hopes for an American stadtholderate would end with it. His failure to proceed with sufficient discretion had caused his otherwise well-laid plans to miscarry. If his henchmen were now to get out of France at all, they must go more secretly than before. If possible, they must avoid sailing on a boat chartered by the American agent, for Stormont kept a very careful watch upon all of Deane's actions. The young man who had been so greatly disappointed by not being able to go to America was destined to provide the way.

(hereafter referred to as A.A.E., Corr. Pol., E.-U.), I, 396; and Lenoir to [Vergennes ?], December 12, *ibid.*, pp. 300–301; cf. American agents to the Committee of Secret Correspondence, January 17, 1777, Wharton, II, 248; Deane to the Committee of Secret Correspondence, January 20, 1777, *ibid.*, p. 252.

[27] Duboismartin to Dekalb, December 14 and 17, 1776, Kapp, pp. 91–93.

[28] Dekalb to Deane, December 17, 1776, A.A.E., Corr. Pol., E.-U., I, 303–7 v., reproduced in Stevens, VI, no. 603.

BIBLIOGRAPHY

On the Comte de Broglie and the Baron Dekalb, see Charles J. Stillé, "Comte de Broglie, the proposed stadtholder of America," *Pennsylvania magazine of history and biography*, I (1888), 369–405; and Friedrich Kapp, *The life of John Kalb, major-general in the Revolutionary army* (New York, 1870). The latter book was originally written in German as *Leben des amerikanischen Generals Johann Kalb* (Stuttgart, 1862). On Kapp's thesis and reliability, see below, p. 149. Doniol's chapter on the departure of Lafayette for America (II, 371–430) was previously published as "Le départ du Marquis de La Fayette pour les États-Unis en 1777," in *Séances et travaux de l'Académie des Sciences Morales et Politiques*, CXXV (1886), 641–75. Doniol is the chief source of information regarding the diplomacy of France during the American Revolution.

Deane's papers were first published by Jared Sparks, *The diplomatic correspondence of the American Revolution* (12 vols.; Boston, 1829–30), but Sparks so often omitted or revised important passages that the later edition by Francis Wharton, *The Revolutionary diplomatic correspondence of the United States* (6 vols.; Washington, 1889), is here used exclusively. Sparks, for example, omitted the passage in the letter of December 6, 1776, wherein Deane suggests Broglie as commander-in-chief of the American army. See also *The Deane papers, correspondence between Silas Deane, his brothers and their business and political associates* ("Collections of the Connecticut Historical Society," Vol. XXIII [Hartford, 1930]), pp. 54–59; and, more important, *The Deane papers, 1774–1778* ("Collections of the New York Historical Society" [5 vols.; New York, 1886–91]). Deane's letter to Robert Morris (May 16, 1777) is perhaps the frankest statement available of the former's attitude toward Lafayette; it is in the papers of the Continental Congress in the Library of Congress.

On Lafayette's relations with the Comte de Broglie, Kapp and Doniol are the principal sources, but these are supplemented by La Marck's narrative in Bacourt's *Correspondance de Mirabeau et La Marck* and the *Mémoires* of Théodore Lameth. The dovetailing of these two accounts, despite certain very striking variations of presentation, is so remarkable as to lead to the suspicion that they are not mutually independent. Yet, since neither book was published until long after the death of both authors, the probabilities are that they are actually quite independent of each other. La Marck, having been closer to the Noailles, is followed here for events that took place at their home; and Lameth, having been closer to Broglie, is accepted as the better witness for what happened at his.

Dekalb's letter to St. Paul, *premier commis* of the department of war, was written in order to refute the charge that he was responsible for Lafayette's departure for America. It is consequently to be used with caution. Furthermore, his memory for dates is not very good, as he places the signing of Lafayette's contract with Deane in November. But it does not seem that Dekalb ever lied deliberately in any of his extant letters and the information he gives is generally trustworthy.

Sparks (*Writings of George Washington*, Vol. V [Boston, 1834]) contains

(Appen. I, pp. 445–56) an account of Lafayette's departure for America which was quoted at great length in the footnotes of Lafayette's *Mémoires* by its editor. Consequently it has been accepted by Lafayette's biographers as having Lafayette's sanction. It may indeed have been the version given to Sparks in 1828, as the editors of Lafayette's papers believed (see *Mémoires*, I, 9 n.), but it is also possible that he copied from a manuscript later put at his disposal by Lafayette, as exactly the same story is told in the second edition of Ducoudray-Holstein, *Memoirs of Gilbert Motier Lafayette*, (Geneva, N.Y., 1835), and Holstein claims in his "Preface" to have received "valuable documents" from Lafayette which enabled him "to present this edition in a more perfect and authentic manner." On the other hand, it is not inconceivable that Holstein plagiarized Sparks. In any case, Sparks's account rather than Holstein's has here been followed, when not corrected by other more reliable sources, because, in the few cases where Holstein's story does not follow his verbatim, Sparks probably has been guided by other information put at his disposal by Lafayette, with whom he was in fairly regular correspondence; Justin Winsor, *Calendar of the Sparks manuscripts in the Harvard College Library* (Cambridge, 1889), p. 19, says that Lafayette himself dictated the Sparks version. Furthermore, in these particular instances Holstein's version appears somewhat fantastic; see below, pp. 159–60.

The pertinent archives of the ministry of foreign affairs at Paris, though it has seemed advisable in many instances to refer directly to them, have been fairly extensively published either by Doniol or by B. F. Stevens, *Facsimiles of manuscripts in European archives relating to America (1773–1783) with descriptions, editorial notes, collations, references and translations* (25 vols.; London, 1889–98).

CHAPTER VII

"Victoire"

WHEN Dekalb and his associates returned to Paris from Le Havre, there was more than Lafayette's disappointment to agitate the Comte de Broglie. He never sent the young man the "advice and instructions" requested,[1] but soon summoned Dekalb and Duboismartin to Ruffec to consider a new plan of action.[2] They agreed that the American expedition must under no circumstances be abandoned. Deane, they hoped, would provide them with another vessel before the group who were to have gone with Dekalb should scatter to all parts of the kingdom.

Deane, however, did nothing during the month of January, 1777, to encourage the Broglie conspiracy. The presence of Franklin in the capital as his colleague made it desirable for him to proceed with greater circumspection than before. If Deane or Dekalb ever informed Franklin of Broglie's aspirations, the knowing old man certainly never became seriously interested in them. Still, on general principles, Franklin did not disapprove of sending French officers to America, though he was more fastidious than Deane had been in this respect.[3] And so, even after his arrival, French soldiers continued to volunteer their services to America, and Deane tried to find the means of transportation for them. Early in February, Dekalb was once

[1] Duboismartin to Dekalb, December 14, 1776, Kapp, pp. 90–91.

[2] *Ibid.*, p. 100. Kapp believed that Lafayette accompanied them to Ruffec, where the decision to buy a boat was reached, and Doniol, II, 376, follows Kapp. It is not impossible that Lafayette went along, though I have encountered no evidence to that effect. But the decision to buy a boat came later; see below, pp. 84–85.

[3] Franklin to Washington, June 13, 1777, A. H. Smyth, *Writings of Benjamin Franklin*, VII (New York, 1906), 59.

more promised a vessel to carry him across the ocean.[4] Unfortunately, no one could tell him exactly when it would sail or who his companions would be, and he had need for precision in both regards.

Meanwhile, Duboismartin had begun to fear that the troop of Broglie's followers who had been so carefully foisted upon Deane in November and December would dwindle away and never be brought together again. His own brother, Lieutenant Duboismartin, who was to have gone with Dekalb as major and aide-de-camp, was getting restless and wished to rejoin his regiment in Santo Domingo. When the secretary urged him to wait for the vessel that Deane was to send to America, the younger Duboismartin could no longer conceal his disgust. He had been a sailor for eleven years before entering the army, and his maritime experience had taught him that, if transportation were not forthcoming from one source, it could be secured from another. He knew, in fact, exactly how it was to be obtained. Why did they have to wait on Deane? If he had any money himself, he'd pay his own passage. Why couldn't a man as rich as the Marquis de Lafayette buy a vessel and take them all over? The idea had never before struck any of Broglie's landlubber friends, but it now seemed a very good one to the older Duboismartin. He asked his brother to put this plan down on paper. This the lieutenant did. Asking the younger man to wait in his room at the Hôtel d'Enghien, the secretary rushed out to find Lafayette.

Over a month had gone by since the Dekalb mission had failed, but the dissatisfied marquis had kept steadily in touch with the Americans in the meantime. As soon as he had learned that Deane was going to send Dekalb off in another ship, he again began to hope that his dream of a major-general's uniform would come true. It was at this juncture that Duboismartin came to see him. The young man agreed to go with him to Lieutenant Duboismartin's lodging, and that evening the three men talked over the new proposal together at the Hôtel d'Enghien. It was easy to see that the negotiations for the purchase of a vessel must be handled with great delicacy. If the

<hr>

[4] Dekalb to St. Paul, November 7, 1777, *American historical review*, XV (1910), 564.

Duc d'Ayen learned of the transaction he would decidedly object. He did not want Lafayette to go to America even if free transportation were provided. He would certainly interfere if it were to cost his son-in-law several thousands of livres. Nevertheless, the marquis gave his consent, and Lieutenant Duboismartain started off for Bordeaux that very night to buy a boat.[5]

Lafayette was elated once more. The old family coat-of-arms now seemed inadequate and colorless to him. He added to it a motto that well expressed his present defiance, *Cur non?* ("Why not?"). The new slogan served both to encourage him when he hesitated and to answer any implied criticism of his actions. His spirits raised by the new vision of success, he went once more to Deane's quarters. "Up to now, sir," he stated in essence, "you have witnessed only my zeal. But now I am going to turn it to some account. I am buying a boat to transport your officers. We must have confidence. I want to share your lot even in the midst of danger."[6] Deane was duly impressed. This was certainly a different type of French adventurer from the hardened soldiers to whom he had become accustomed. The virus of idealism, to which Lafayette's adolescence rendered him particularly susceptible, was apparently beginning now to take effect.

Fearing to be discovered going in and out of Deane's offices, Lafayette thereafter kept in touch with the American headquarters at the Hôtel d'Hambourg on the Rue Jacob through Deane's secretary, William Carmichael. Once, when Carmichael wrote him to come to his rooms for a consultation, the cautious lad invited Carmichael to his house instead.[7] That was the first of several clandestine meetings between the two men, most often in the dead of night. By day Lafayette would sometimes pick up Carmichael in his carriage and they would talk

---

[5] For the foregoing episode, see statement by Lieutenant Duboismartin, Maryland Historical Society, Baltimore, portfolio 9; and the letter of Lieutenant Duboismartin to Lafayette, [October, 1823], *ibid.*

[6] *Mémoires*, I, 12.

[7] Lafayette to Carmichael, [*ca.* February, 1777], Library of Congress, House of Representatives papers, no. 95; cf. Lupton to Eden, April 8, 1777, Stevens, *Facsimiles*, VII, no. 681.

about the young man's argosy to the beat of horses' hoofs upon the stones of the Paris streets.

The marquis soon became attached to his older adviser and grew more and more conscious of his newer ideals. Some of the American secretary's earnestness for the cause of the young nation in whose behalf the French nobleman was preparing to make so many sacrifices began to awaken within him. For the first time he spoke seriously of a zeal not only for the independence of the revolting colonies but for their happiness and glory as well.[8] Even in his conversations with Deane, when trying to impress the gullible American agent with his qualifications for a high post in the Continental Army, Lafayette had— quite fittingly—exhibited only what Deane reported to Congress as "zeal for the liberty of our provinces"; and it was altogether natural for a French aristocrat, bred to envy of the Briton's empire, to cherish the idea of independence for England's finest colonies. But, in the presence of his new-found friend, Lafayette began to feel the contagion of his devotion. It was merely a slight infection as yet, and even the young victim probably could not tell how much of it was real and how much intended only for display, but out of it was to grow great ardor and conviction.

What happened at the Hôtel d'Hambourg was of such immense interest to the French authorities that the comings and goings of a well-connected youth could not long be concealed from inquisitive eyes. The police of Paris were soon fully aware of what was going on, and the boy's family also had their suspicions roused. They took the matter up informally with Maurepas, believing that official action might serve as a more effective check upon the young man's plans than family interference. Maurepas sent his protégé, the Prince de Montbarey, a high official in the war office, to speak to Lafayette. The lad confessed what he had intended to do, but promised repeatedly to give up his plans in deference to the minister's wishes. Despite his apparent docility, however, Lafayette did not con-

---

[8] Lafayette to Carmichael, [February 11, 1777], L.C., House of Rep. papers, no. 98; cf. Lupton to [Eden], April 8, 1777, Stevens, VII, no. 681.

vince Montbarey. The prince reported both to Maurepas and to St. Germain that he was convinced Lafayette would persist, but the ministers felt that they had done enough to preserve appearances and washed their hands of the matter for the moment.[9]

Nevertheless, the danger that the government might again interfere with their plans now seemed all too imminent to Lafayette and his friends, and they determined to take additional precautions. It was agreed that the young intriguer should go to England. This could easily be arranged, as the Prince de Poix had long been planning to visit Adrienne's uncle, the Marquis de Noailles, French ambassador at London, and had asked Lafayette to go with him. Not desiring to be too far from the Hôtel d'Hambourg, Lafayette had at first hesitated to accept this invitation. It was now thought that to continue to refuse would give further ground for suspicion regarding his plans, while to agree would be to cover up his real intentions. It was perfectly natural that the two cousins should go to see a relative who was ambassador in a foreign country. The very fact that that country was the one against which one of them was supposed to have evil designs would throw the police authorities off the scent. Word could easily be delivered to the truant when all would be in readiness.

The plans for the English voyage materialized in February during carnival week. It was decided that Lafayette and the Prince de Poix should leave Paris on the Sunday following Mardi Gras. Meanwhile a dreary succession of balls and dances from which the queen did not return until dawn, and no gentleman of the court dared depart before her, consumed the eager young man's time. The prospect of a first visit to a foreign country held no thrill for him now. His heart and mind were fixed upon what was to happen in France. He hoped particularly to receive word from Bordeaux before he left. Finally, on February 11, he heard from the younger Duboismartin. The lieutenant had met with great success.

The outstanding shipowners of France were the firm of

---

[9] *Mémoires de M. le Prince de Montbarey*, II, 261–63.

Reculès de Basmarein et Raimbaux of Bordeaux. Duboismartin had already had dealings with this house. Pierre de Basmarein, the head of the firm, was a young man who had invested heavily in trade with the American insurgents and was ready to do so again, not only because he was sympathetic with their cause, but also because he believed it would be profitable. Duboismartin pointed out to him the danger of the new undertaking. The family of Lafayette and the court might create insurmountable difficulties if they found out about the transaction. Basmarein, nevertheless, was willing to take the risk. He had a good boat named the "Victoire," commanded by the experienced Captain Le Boursier. It weighed two hundred and twenty tons, was armed with two cannons, had a crew of thirty men, and had already made several trips to America. The boat and its cargo, Basmarein claimed, were worth 112,000 livres. He would dispose of it to Lafayette for 40,000 livres in cash and the balance by June.[10] The "Victoire" would be ready to sail by the middle of March. This was welcome news, indeed, to the impatient Lafayette.

On the same day that this information arrived, Carmichael, too, wanted very much to see the would-be major-general in order to arrange a meeting with Franklin and Deane. Great as was the marquis' eagerness to impart the latest tidings, he could not accept, for it was Shrove Tuesday and the queen's Mardi Gras ball was to finish off the week's festivities. Lafayette was expected to be present. He promised Carmichael, however, to take him for a carriage ride the next day in order to talk over their plans.[11] Of all the dances and dinners that Lafayette had attended in his short life, this one must have struck the budding idealist, hiding his great secret in his breast, as the most frivolous and ill-timed. The rest of the court, however, greatly enjoyed themselves. They danced at the queen's from five to

[10] Dekalb to Mme Dekalb, April 1, 1777, Vicomte de Colleville, *Les missions secrètes du Général-Major Baron de Kalb et son rôle dans la Guerre de l'Indépendance Américaine* (Paris, 1885), p. 132.

[11] Lafayette to Carmichael, [February 11, 1777], L.C., House of Rep. papers, no. 98. For a discussion of the possibility that it was about this time that Lafayette signed his definitive contract with Deane, see below, Appen. V.

nine, then seated themselves at supper, and immediately afterward went off with Her Majesty to the Bal de l'Opéra, from which they did not return until six o'clock in the morning.[12]

Whether or not Lafayette kept his engagement with Carmichael the next morning, he did not make Franklin's acquaintance that day or on the ones that followed, and he started out for England with the Prince de Poix on the succeeding Sunday (February 16). They arrived at his uncle's embassy a few days later. Lafayette did not find England itself very enjoyable. He could not speak a word of English and he met only a few people who could talk French. One of these was Horace Walpole, who was a dinner guest at the Marquis de Noailles' home and saw the ambassador's two nephews there. He was much impressed with the Prince de Poix, but failed even to mention the Marquis de Lafayette in his letters to his devoted French correspondent, Mme du Deffand.[13] Among the others whom the young American partisan encountered were several men who were leading the resistance to the revolting colonies. At the opera one night he met General Clinton, who had recently distinguished himself at the Battle of Long Island. He danced at the home of Lord George Germain, minister of the colonies, where he made the acquaintance of Lord Rawdon, who had just returned from New York. He was also presented to King George by his uncle, the ambassador. With all these men he tried to be as discreet as possible. Nevertheless, he could not make a complete secret of his sympathies, and on one occasion openly defended the Americans, frankly expressing his satisfaction with the recent news of Washington's victory at Trenton. This candid avowal of his views brought him an invitation to dinner with the Earl of Shelburne, one of the leaders of the pro-American faction in Parliament. It was probably here that began his singular friendship with Richard Fitzpatrick, Whig member of Parliament, whom he was to meet again as a soldier in America and who on several

[12] Mercy-Argenteau to Maria Theresa, February 15, 1777, Arneth and Geffroy, *Correspondance secrète entre Marie-Thérèse et Mercy-Argenteau*, III, 20.

[13] Mme du Deffand to Walpole, March 23 and 31, 1777, Lescure (ed.), *Correspondance complète de la Marquise du Deffand avec ses amis*, II (Paris, 1865), 595–96, 597.

future occasions was to be in a position to do him a service.[14]
Feeling somewhat awkward about the delicate position in which
he was placing his unsuspecting uncle, and anxious to appear
not to have spied upon the English, Lafayette declined an opportunity to inspect the naval armaments which were being prepared at Portsmouth for the war in America. He might have
spared himself this gesture, however, for some Englishmen long
continued to believe that not only he but also the Marquis de
Noailles took a dishonorable advantage of their privileged position on this occasion.[15]

As a matter of fact, Lafayette was not at all interested in
England; his attention was fixed upon Bordeaux. He learned
little of the English language, and less about the people in the
short time that he spent among these hated British. His only
comments about them later were to point out how inferior Englishmen, and especially Englishwomen, were to the Americans.[16]
Something of greater importance destroyed his tranquillity of
mind and kept him preoccupied. He had left Adrienne and her
family under the impression that he would return home after
his little jaunt in England. Actually, if his plans reached the
fruition he so earnestly desired, he would not see them again
until, redeemed and glorious, he came back from the American
war. How could he make his peace with his wife and his father-
in-law? Distance lent him courage, and he decided to do by
letter what he had not dared to do in person. After three weeks
in London, he composed a careful letter to the Duc d'Ayen,
which nevertheless betrayed the conflict of emotions rising
within him. Pride over his high rank and devotion to his newly
discovered cause struggled for supremacy in his thoughts as he
wrote. "You will be surprised," he said, "at what I have to tell
you, ... but my word has been given and you would not respect me if I broke it. . . . . I have found a unique opportunity
to distinguish myself and to learn my profession. I am a general
officer in the army of the United States of America. My zeal for

---

[14] Lafayette to Mme Lafayette, April 28, 1778, *Mémoires*, I, 170–71, and note.

[15] Cf. *Journal and correspondence of William, first Lord Auckland*, II, 421 and 462.

[16] Lafayette to Mme Lafayette, June 19, 1777, *Mémoires*, I, 93–94.

their cause and my sincerity have won their confidence. For my part, I have done all that I can for them, and their interests will always be dearer to me than my own." He went on to explain that he was expecting news from his friends at any moment. As soon as he heard from them he intended to leave London, and, without stopping at Paris, embark upon a vessel which he had bought, accompanied by the Baron Dekalb, "major-general in the United States service like myself," and several other excellent officers. "I am filled with joy," he concluded, "at having found so beautiful a chance to accomplish something and to learn. I know very well that I am making enormous sacrifices and that it will hurt me more than anyone else to leave my family, my friends, you, my dear papa, because I love you more tenderly than anyone ever has loved before. But this voyage is not very long. People make longer ones every day for pleasure alone and besides I hope to return more worthy of all those who will be so good as to miss me."[17] It was a pathetic epistle, revealing a diffident adolescent, who, though determined to follow his own decisions and proud of being a general, yet pleaded like a mischievous child that his family be not angry with him for going away without consulting them. But before Lafayette could send his letter off, the long-expected message arrived from Paris. Duboismartin had kept the Broglie clique regularly informed of what was going on at Bordeaux. At last, negotiations with Basmarein reached the point where all was ready for Lafayette's final consent, and Dekalb sent the errant marquis the word to return. It was now the second week in March. They were already delayed longer than they had at first intended.

The signal to leave England came to Lafayette at an inopportune moment. He had been in London several weeks and was expected once more to go with his wife's uncle to court. It seemed strange that now suddenly, after so brief a stay, the young man should so emphatically wish to return, especially without his companion. He explained to the somewhat inconvenienced ambassador that he had an important commission to

<hr>

[17] Lafayette to Duc d'Ayen, London, March 9, 1777, *Mémoires*, I, 82–84.

perform in Paris and would return. Noailles was obliged to pretend at the king's reception that his absent nephew was sick. Leaving his wife's relatives somewhat discomfited behind him, the eager youth started out for France as rapidly as he could go. With the letter to his "dear papa" in his baggage, he boarded a fast boat, recrossed the straits, and, forgetting a horrible attack of seasickness as soon as he landed, hastened off to the suburb of Chaillot, where Dekalb resided.

How narrowly Lafayette's plans had come to being discovered while he was in England the young adventurer never knew. At least two English spies had been allowed to learn of his intentions. Among the personages Lafayette had visited in London was the American Dr. Edward Bancroft, generally believed to be a friend of the insurgents, but actually in secret correspondence with both sides.[18] Bancroft, however, did not divulge Lafayette's secret for the present. At about the same time Carmichael unwittingly jeopardized the success of the very plot he had labored so hard to foster. He was extremely anxious to have some American accompany Lafayette's expedition. All the rest of the marquis' companions were to be Frenchmen with the single exception of the thoroughly Gallicized Dekalb, and none but the "baron" spoke any English. Carmichael had hoped to induce a certain George Lupton to go along as Lafayette's aide, little knowing that Lupton was more friendly to the English than the Americans. Fortunately Carmichael mentioned no names and therefore Lupton learned the identity of the persons involved only when it was too late. Lupton preferred to remain in Europe, and so, at the last moment, Carmichael invited his young friend, Edmund Brice, to go and Brice accepted. Brice was entirely reliable.[19]

Carmichael had informed Brice that the gentlemen he was to accompany would leave Paris no later than March 5. It was

<hr />

[18] S. F. Bemis, "British secret service and the French-American alliance," *American historical review*, XXIX (1924), 474–95; Lewis Einstein, *Divided loyalties* (Boston, 1933), pp. 3–15.

[19] Carmichael to Brice, Paris, February 20, 1777, Stevens, I, no. 29; see also *ibid.*, II, nos. 141 and 143; [Lupton] to [Eden], April 24, 1777, *ibid.*, VII, no. 686; Lafayette to Carmichael, April 19, 1777, L.C., House of Rep. papers, no. 99.

actually about a week after that date when Lafayette returned to France. For a few days (March 13–16) he stayed in hiding at Chaillot. He lived anonymously, scarcely daring to leave his lodgings, at the home of a gardener. To his host he was known only as "the gentleman on the first floor."[20] He saw Dekalb frequently. Basmarein also came to see him, and the details of the purchase of the "Victoire" were definitely concluded.[21] Lafayette found it difficult to raise 40,000 livres without consulting his father-in-law, but managed to borrow enough from several friends, overcoming the hesitation of the shipowner, whose ideals had to struggle against his fears for his profits, by promising protection and friendship for the future.

Summoned by Dekalb, Carmichael also came to Chaillot.[22] It was necessary to decide upon the men to send to America on the "Victoire." Deane was more cautious now than he had been before the arrival of Franklin, and the Comte de Broglie had also been quite careful recently not to show his hand. Consequently, besides Dekalb and Duboismartin, only three others of the original Dekalb expedition were included among those who were decided upon to sail on the "Victoire" for America. Seven new names were added, making, with Lafayette, a total of thirteen. This list, apparently already signed by Deane, was now approved by Lafayette and Dekalb. It was antedated December 7, 1776, in order to make it conform as nearly as possible with the original agreements with Dekalb and Lafayette and to have it appear that it had preceded the arrival of Franklin.[23] When all was in readiness, Carmichael gave the two major-generals letters of introduction to several members of Congress for

[20] Dekalb to Carmichael, March 14, [1777], L.C., House of Rep. papers, no. 93.

[21] Basmarein to Lafayette, [1782], in Robert Castex, "Armateur de La Fayette, Pierre de Basmarein," *Revue des questions historiques,* LIII (1925), 123–24.

[22] Dekalb to Carmichael, March 14, [1777], L.C., House of Rep. Papers, no. 93. Lafayette (*Mémoires,* I, 13) says "*les Américains,*" but Deane probably and Franklin certainly were not among them; see John Bigelow, "Unpublished letters of Benjamin Franklin," *Century magazine,* XXI (1886), 265. See also Stormont to Weymouth, Paris, April 3, 1777, P.R.O., S.P., France 78/302, not numbered, and cf. Franklin to Washington, Passy, March 5, 1780, Smyth, VIII, 27–28. In *Mémoires,* I, 69, Lafayette mentions only Carmichael.

[23] See below, Append. V.

themselves and others of their party.[24] Deane provided Lafayette with a letter of recommendation to the house of Robert Morris for his banking needs, and later wrote to George Washington as commander-in-chief and John Hancock as president of Congress, commending both Lafayette and Dekalb to their particular attention.[25] In all of these missives the American agents took special pains to emphasize the great wealth and important family connections of the Marquis de Lafayette.

Everything so far had passed off most successfully and Lafayette itched to tell someone about it. Adrienne would have been just the right confidant, but, as Gilbert told Dekalb, to go to see her would mean a scene of tenderness and affliction which he preferred to avoid.[26] Ségur and Noailles were just the ones to hear his boast. This was his long-awaited chance to triumph over them, and they could besides be trusted to keep his secret. One morning at seven o'clock he burst into Ségur's room, carefully shut the door, and, seating himself close to Ségur's bed, told him how he had bought the "Victoire" and was on his way. Ségur was both amazed and jealous, but without waiting to enjoy his triumph, Lafayette rushed off to break the news to Noailles.[27] Then he returned to Chaillot. At noon of the same day (March 16, 1777) Dekalb and he started off for Bordeaux in a carriage which two days earlier Lafayette had taken the precaution to have sent to Dekalb's stables.

A few minutes' ride brought them to Paris and hard by the Noailles hôtel. Lafayette could not go on without writing a word of farewell to his family. They stopped the carriage long enough for him to scribble a brief note to Adrienne. He told her how much it hurt him to have to leave her. The thought of her sorrow was his chief regret, he almost tearfully said, but, having

[24] Carmichael to Tilghman, March 17, 1777, photostat in the Gardner-Ball Collection, Indiana University Library; Carmichael to Richard Henry Lee, Paris, March, 1777, Kapp, pp. 301-2.

[25] Deane to Robert Morris, March 16, 1776, *The Deane papers*, II ("Collections of the New York Historical Society for the year 1887"), 24. Cf. Deane to Dekalb, March 22, 1777, *ibid.*, pp. 29-30; and the drafts of letters to Washington and Hancock, April 5, 1777, *ibid.*, pp. 39-40.

[26] Dekalb to St. Paul, November 7, 1777, *loc. cit.*, p. 564.	[27] Ségur, I, 107-8.

given his promise, he felt that he must keep it. The Duc d'Ayen would give her the details about his plans.[28] To the letter he had written at London to his father-in-law, he now added a short postscript explaining that he was too pressed for time to appear in person and asking to be remembered to his "Aunt" and "Uncle" Lusignem. When both letters were sent off, the two companions entered the carriage once more and continued their journey. They arrived at Bordeaux on March 19, having stopped for only one night's rest en route.[29] The road seemed clear ahead. They hoped to be on the high seas before anyone could interfere.

BIBLIOGRAPHY

See bibliography for chap. vi. On the purchase of the "Victoire," the principal sources are statements drawn up some years afterward by François-Augustin-Martin de Barbezieux, generally known as Captain Duboismartin, though actually in 1777 a lieutenant. These are now to be found in the Maryland Historical Society at Baltimore. These documents are not altogether reliable, as they were intended to show the author's right to some sort of payment by Lafayette for his part in bringing the marquis to America. Nevertheless, what they say about the arrangements for the purchase of the "Victoire" fits in too well with other available data to leave much room for doubt as to their general truthfulness in this regard.

On Lafayette's career in England, his *Mémoires* are the best source, though these may be supplemented by Sparks's *Writings of George Washington*, Vol. V, Appen. I, and by the *Espion anglais ou correspondance secrète entre Milord All'Eye et Milord All'Ear*, VI (London, 1783), 67–71 (under date of May 26, 1777).

On Basmarein's part in the sale of the "Victoire," see Robert Castex, "Armateur de La Fayette, Pierre de Basmarein, d'après des documents inédits," *Revue des questions historiques*, CII (1925), 78–133. This article is based on the papers of the firm which Pierre de Basmarein headed, some of which are now in the Stuart W. Jackson Collection, Yale University Library, and the Gardner-Ball Collection, Indiana University Library. Sam Maxwell, "Embarquement de Lafayette à Bordeaux," *Revue philomathique de Bordeaux et du Sud-Ouest*, X (1907), 385–95, is based exclusively upon Doniol's volumes.

William Carmichael's granddaughter submitted a memorial to the Twenty-sixth Congress, first session (December 2, 1839—July 21, 1840), for the adjustment of her claims as sole heir to her grandfather. The letters of Lafayette to Carmichael were inclosed with the memorial. They were transferred to the

[28] A copy of this letter in the hand of Mme de Lafayette forms a part of the collection gathered by M. Emmanuel Fabius, autograph merchant of Paris: see page 15 above.

[29] Dekalb to Mme Dekalb, March 20, 1777 (though here erroneously dated "30 mai 1776"), Colleville, p. 124.

Library of Congress in 1910 in accordance with a resolution in 1900 authoriz-ing the clerk of the House of Representatives to send to the Library such papers of the House files as he saw fit. They are contained in Carton I of the House of Representative papers, 1775–1819, and known as the "Carmichael papers." These letters have also been quoted and translated by Elizabeth S. Kite, "Lafayette and his companions on the 'Victoire' (Part I)," *Records of the American Catholic Historical Society*, XLV (1934), 17–22, 29–32, though with some inaccuracies of dating and transliteration.

The Dekalb letters reprinted in Colleville, *Missions secrètes du Baron de Kalb*, were taken from the papers in the possession of Dekalb's granddaughter. Colleville was, however, an extremely bad editor and inadequately informed regarding Dekalb's career. Consequently the Kapp edition of the letters has always been cited here except, as sometimes happens, when Colleville gives more of the letter than Kapp reproduced.

CHAPTER VIII

The First Escape

WHEN the letters of the fugitive husband and son-in-law reached the Noailles hôtel, they were received with conflicting emotions. Lafayette's wife and his mother-in-law were both deeply fond of the errant lad. To poor Adrienne, tenderly devoted to her husband and expecting her second child within a few months, his unannounced departure was a rude shock. Her mother, fearing for her health, broke the news gently and consoled her as best she could. The two women shared their sorrow in quiet understanding. But the rest of the family were furious. They accused Gilbert of folly, inordinate ambition, and vain prodigality. They railed against Dekalb, Basmarein, Deane, and others, whom they thought responsible for his fatuous enterprise. Ségur alone was secretly amused at their chagrin and rejoiced at his friend's success.

Adrienne, despite her grief, refused to join in the reproaches of her family. With studied patience she prepared to wait for news of her quixotic husband and helped her mother to be useful to him in every way she could. Adrienne's sisters likewise endeavored to soften the blow for the expectant mother. All unawares, the ladies of the house really approved of the offending lad. But Adrienne's other relatives thought it strange that she should not be resentful. Only the duchess understood her silence, and Basmarein alone, whom she reproached for his share in her husband's adventure, saw her tears.[1] Otherwise she preferred that people think her phlegmatic and even a little childish,

[1] Basmarein to Lafayette, [1782], Castex, "Pierre de Basmarein," *Revue des questions historiques*, CII (1925), 124.

lest their sympathy for her make them feel more bitter toward her venturesome husband.

The Duc d'Ayen determined that the wild enterprise must be stopped, and lost no time in placing the situation before the ministers. Perhaps Maurepas was displeased that the young man should have broken the promise given to Montbarey. But it was even more disquieting that Stormont had recently made several complaints about violations of French neutrality. This new escapade bade fair to become more serious than at first glance would have been thought possible. A son-in-law of the Noailles and nephew of the ambassador to the court of St. James, fresh from his presentation to the king of England, would be looked upon by the English envoy in a different light from the ordinary soldier-adventurer who went off to America. Stormont's protests would certainly be more vigorous on this occasion than hitherto.

Before Stormont learned of what had happened, however, Maurepas decided upon a course of action. D'Ayen, his sister, and her husband, the Comte de Tessé, had for some time been planning a tour of Italy. D'Ayen and Maurepas agreed that Lafayette should be ordered to go to Italy with them, and thus be prevented from carrying out his project. That would give his American ardor a chance to cool off. Not knowing to which port the young man had gone and fearing that the lad's boat might have already reached the high seas, the minister dispatched a vessel to catch up with him and deliver these commands.[2]

Maurepas acted thus only to preserve the appearance of neutrality. Yet he did not wish actually to be neutral. He made no effort to stop the "Victoire" and the other French officers on her. He merely hoped to please the Noailles family and to avoid the open scandal that the escape of one of them to America would occasion. In fact, the "Victoire" had not been the only boat at Bordeaux which was preparing to sail to America. Instructions had been sent to the port officials as early as March 8 to watch two such vessels. The harbor authorities had expressed the opinion that if the government really wanted

[2] See n. 12 below.

to stop Bordeaux ships from bringing aid to England's revolting
colonies, it would be necessary to station an armed cruiser at
the mouth of the Garonne River. Though there had been ample
time for such action, this had not been done.[3] The ministry had
clearly not been anxious to stop the departure of French officers
for America in that instance. It was now interested only in saving its face as far as Lafayette was concerned. The king himself
made no secret of the fact that he was profoundly shocked that
a man of Lafayette's position in society should go to the assistance of rebels. He was apparently unconcerned about others
who committed the same offense.

Stormont and a secret English agent known as Colonel Smith
watched this reaction to Lafayette's tactics with increasing suspicion. Both believed that the French ministers had encouraged the marquis and other French volunteers. Before Smith
discovered that Lafayette had actually left France, he wrote
to his government that a young man whose name his informant
so mangled in the pronunciation that "there was no guessing
what it was," had arranged to leave France for service in the
American army. Smith's statement was used as the basis of a
report by the foreign office which was later submitted to George
III. Depending upon this and other sources of information, the
author of this report gave the culprit's name correctly, and denounced the French "spirit of duplicity," whereby "French
officers are refused leave to serve in the rebel army, but are always permitted, and even encouraged to go."[4] This exactly described Stormont's point of view, likewise, but as yet he made
no formal protest to the French government. He waited to see
what would be the outcome of the efforts to stop Lafayette.[5]

Meanwhile, Dekalb and Lafayette had reached Bordeaux.
But all was not in readiness, as they had hoped. They were a
few days ahead of the rest of their companions; and the "Vic-

[3] Doniol, II, 382 n.

[4] Stevens, VII, no. 670, and III, no. 248; cf. George III to Lord North, March 28,
1777, *ibid.*, VII, no. 671.

[5] Stormont to Weymouth, April 2, 1777, P.R.O., S.P., France 78/302, no. 58.

toire" was not yet prepared to sail. It looked as if they would have to lose several valuable days in idle waiting. Lafayette was worried and Dekalb annoyed. To make matters worse, the marquis, fearing that the Paris authorities might now have time to act before he could get away, confided his secret to Dekalb. He confessed that he did not yet have the Duc d'Ayen's consent to his enterprise, and that his father-in-law might therefore call upon the ministers to prohibit his voyage. Dekalb was distinctly surprised and greatly displeased, since the boy had hitherto consistently maintained that he had his family's approval. They agreed that the best thing to do was to send a courier to Paris with orders to call upon the Vicomte de Coigny, one of Lafayette's friends; learn from him the effect of Lafayette's conduct upon his family and the ministers; and, if possible, "prevent an interdict from issuing." The courier started out from Bordeaux on March 20. "Nothing is more uncertain," the restless Dekalb wrote his wife, "than this voyage. . . . . The marquis is greatly disturbed by the delay and I think he is right. It is possible that we shall not sail."[6]

While waiting for the courier's return and for the "Victoire" to get ready, Lafayette, pretending to have come on a visit, stayed at the home of his wife's great-uncle, the Marshal de Mouchy, who lived at Bordeaux as lieutenant-governor of Basse-Guyenne. Without being certain whether steps would be taken to prevent the departure of the "Victoire," Lafayette recognized the possibility that he himself might not be permitted to embark. Therefore, though Dekalb registered with the embarkation officers under his own name shortly after he reached Bordeaux (March 21), Lafayette signed only a day later and under an equivocal name—Gilbert du Motier, Chevalier de Chavaillac. Since Chavaillac was an archaic form of Chavaniac, it was a name to which he was perfectly entitled, though few would have recognized him by it. He described himself on the embarkation certificate as tall, blonde, and twenty years of age. While he was tall compared to most contemporary Frenchmen, his hair was reddish, and his age was nineteen. By this slight deception he hoped to avoid detection.

[6] March 20, 1777, Colleville, pp. 124–25; Kapp, pp. 103–4.

None the less the boy's worst fears were soon confirmed. Coigny sent back the courier almost immediately with the report that Lafayette's relations, the ministers, and the king had all evinced distinct displeasure, and were taking definite measures to stop him. There was even some talk of a *lettre de cachet*, a secret royal order to imprison the misled youth and keep him out of mischief.

The courier arrived at Bordeaux on the morning of March 25. He was just in the nick of time. A few minutes' delay would have caused him to miss Lafayette. By March 24 all of Deane's officers agreed upon at Chaillot, as well as Brice and some others, had duly registered,[7] and the "Victoire" had anchored in the roadstead at Pauillac. The winds were unfavorable, however, until March 25. That morning the "Victoire" was ready, and they decided to sail without waiting for the courier's return from Paris. He caught them just as they were getting into the launch that was to take them out to the "Victoire."[8] Lafayette tore open Coigny's letter and read it as they rowed toward the larger vessel. When he had finished, he was thoroughly agitated. A *lettre de cachet* was a very serious matter. With one of these secret orders the king might imprison anyone for any length of time without specifying the reason, and he frequently used them to keep the sons of well-known families from disgracing themselves.

When Dekalb learned what was the trouble, he advised his anxious companion to yield and to sell the "Victoire." He was distinctly provoked at the delay that would thereby result, yet did not think that he ought to urge his young friend to disregard the wishes of his family and his king. But Lafayette decided it was too late to turn back now. Besides, they had nothing but the Vicomte de Coigny's version of what was going on. The actuality might be something rather different. Since they were already on their way, they must at least get out of France. The nearest Spanish ports were not very far off. They might go there and await further developments or decide upon another course of action.[9] The need for haste was pressing, since it was

[7] See Appen. VI below.   [8] Dekalb to Mme Dekalb, April 6, 1777, Kapp, p. 105.
[9] *Ibid.*, and Dekalb to St. Paul, *loc. cit.*, pp. 564-65.

quite plain that, if Coigny should make known Lafayette's presence at Bordeaux, a governmental messenger would be sent after him. Dispatching a courier of his own to secure more definite information than Coigny had furnished, Lafayette determined to sail for San Sebastian in Spain.[10]

The "Victoire," after it had picked up the two major-generals, sailed down the Garonne River. The next day they were at Verdon, at the mouth of the harbor, and two days later they made port at Los Pasajes.[11] Meanwhile a courier sent from Paris to stop Lafayette had reached Bordeaux.[12] He arrived only a few hours after Lafayette's boat had disappeared beyond the horizon. There was nothing left for the courier to do but to refer the orders for Lafayette to M. de Fumel, the commandant of the port, and leave him to decide upon the next step to take.

BIBLIOGRAPHY

The principal source for what happened at Bordeaux is the correspondence of Dekalb with his wife, published by Kapp, pp. 103–6, and the letter of Dekalb to St. Paul in the *American historical review*, XV (1910), 562–67. For the effect of Lafayette's conduct on the Noailles family and on public opinion, see Lasteyrie, *Madame de Lafayette;* Bacourt, *Correspondance de la Marck;* Ségur, *Mémoires;* and the correspondence of Stormont in the Public Record Office, London. A question easily arises as to the degree of credibility that should be attributed to Stormont's dispatches. His unenviable position at Paris required him to be suspicious. He was therefore likely to report rumor as fact. On the other hand, he was usually well informed, he made a visible effort to distinguish between reliable and unreliable evidence, and his reports were careful and sober. In general, his testimony as to what took place between him and the French government has been accepted here at its face value. On that point he would be particularly careful to tell the truth to his home office. Of his comments concerning the stealthiness of Maurepas and Vergennes and the guilty maneuvers of Broglie, only such have been repeated

[10] Dekalb to Mme Dekalb, March 26, 1777, Kapp, p. 104.

[11] See Appen. VII below.

[12] There is some question as to whether it was a boat rather than a courier that was sent after Lafayette. Cf. the letters of Goltz to Frederick II of Prussia, April 6 and 13, 1777, Preussisches Geheimes Staatsarchiv, Rep. XI, Frankreich 89, fasc. 250, fols. 81 and 87; and Stormont to Weymouth, April 2, 1777, P.R.O., S.P., France 78/302, no. 58. Stormont thought there were two couriers, as well as a boat, but it is evident that one of them is Lafayette's courier who went from Bordeaux to Paris and back again at the marquis' orders; and the boat, having been sent before it was known that Lafayette went to Bordeaux, would have raced not to Bordeaux, but to the trade channels between France and the West Indies, where French vessels bound for America generally called.

as are corroborated by other sources, unless it was to portray Stormont's own reactions.

The Baron de Goltz, who was Prussian envoy to Paris, likewise mentioned Lafayette in several letters to Frederick the Great; these are now in the Preussisches Geheimes Staatsarchiv in Berlin-Dahlem. Catherine the Great's informant sent her the same reports as appeared in the *Journal de Métra;* see Lescure (ed.), *Correspondance secrète sur Louis XVI,* I, 40–43, 45, and 55. The newspapers of the day (*Gazette de Leyde,* under date of April 15 and 18, and May 13 and 16; *Gazette d'Amsterdam,* under date of May 13, 1777; the *Courrier de l'Europe,* quoted by Jacques Kayser, *La vie de La Fayette* [Paris, 1928], p. 25), and the chroniclers (*Journal de Métra,* IV, 264–67, 384; *Espion anglais,* VI, 52, 67–71) all carry stories that agree in the large, but contain conflicting and mistaken details with which rumor embellished the tale.

From this point on, Lafayette's *Mémoires* and the account he furnished Sparks become unreliable, since his excitement was so great as to color his subsequent memory of what happened and to make it, if not altogether inaccurate, at least extremely incomplete and one-sided. The very clever *They knew the Washingtons: letters from a French soldier with Lafayette and from his family in Virginia,* translated by the Princess Radziwill (Indianapolis, 1926), is apparently a work of fiction, as are also the letters in Princess Radziwill, "Washington and Lafayette," *Century magazine,* CXII (1926), 271–78.

CHAPTER IX

Twisting the Lion's Tail

AT PARIS, after the arrival of Lafayette's courier to the Vicomte de Coigny, the news of Lafayette's escape became common property. The unusually well-informed gossips at Mme du Deffand's salon learned on March 31 about his departure from Bordeaux,[1] though it was not until April 2 that official circles became excited about it. Lafayette suddenly stepped out of insignificance into fame. That one of France's richest and best connected young men, aristocrat by birth and training, courtier and absentee landlord, should go off across the seas to join insurgents and republicans was an exciting topic of conversation. It amused some and annoyed others, but all were agreed that this was no ordinary adventurer. This rebel was a man who had every reason to be content—a pretty wife, a large income, a proud title, "in fact everything which can make life agreeable and dear."[2] One noblewoman wrote to her son that this M. de Lafayette must be a madman: "Go to help the insurgents! . . . . How I pity his mother!"[3] But in general the Paris ladies admired the young man. "It's undoubtedly an act of folly," wrote the faithful Mme du Deffand to Horace Walpole, "but one which does him no dishonor and which, on the contrary, is characterized by courage and the desire for glory. People praise him more than they blame him."[4] Even

---

[1] Mme du Deffand to Walpole, March 31, 1777, *Correspondance de la Marquise du Deffand*, II, 597–98; cf. *The last journals of Horace Walpole*, ed. A. Francis Steuart, II (London, 1910), 19–20 (under date of April 9, 1777).

[2] Chevalier de Marais to his mother, quoted by B. Tuckerman, "The enlistment of Lafayette, 1776," *New Princeton review*, II (1886), 376–88.

[3] *Ibid.*   [4] Du Deffand, *Correspondance*, II, 598.

the queen was said to applaud the marquis' act and to be incit-
ing to emulate his example the same young noblemen who
recently had joined in her mockery of him.[5] And, according to
Maurepas, one of the ladies at court maintained that if the Duc
d'Ayen thwarted such a son-in-law in such an enterprise, he
need not expect to marry off his other daughters.[6]

It was not about his unmarried daughters alone, however,
that the Duc d'Ayen was disturbed. He was more concerned
about the lad who was wasting his money on a cause of which
his king did not approve and who might bring disgrace upon the
family and particularly the Marquis de Noailles, who had just
presented him to the king of England. Moreover, there was the
possibility that he might fall into the hands of the British. That
was a horrible thought. Yet since the lad had apparently made
good his escape, his father-in-law felt that there was nothing
he could do except to send orders after him to return. He wrote
a letter to the wilful boy, and asked Gérard, Vergennes' first
secretary, to have Deane forward it to Lafayette together with
letters from other members of the family. They informed the
fugitive of the king's displeasure and the orders for his recall.
D'Ayen counted upon the department of foreign affairs to use
its influence with the guilty Deane to effect the boy's return and
thus repair the damage already done.[7]

If the king of France and his prime minister could side with
an irate father-in-law to prevent an ambitious young Frenchman from violating the neutrality of his country, and if the
French foreign office could be expected—openly, at least—to co-
operate with them, it was not because of any love for the English at Louis XVI's court. The collapse of the British Empire
would bring only great rejoicing to France. Some Frenchmen
dared to hope that the rebellion in America might lead to the
re-establishment of French domination in the Western Hemi-

[5] Wentworth to Suffolk, April 14, 1777, Stevens, *Facsimiles*, III, no. 250.

[6] Stormont to Weymouth, May 7, 1777, P.R.O., S.P., France 78/302, no. 82.

[7] Cf. Deane to Gérard, April 2, 1777, *Deane papers*, II, 37; Deane to Vergennes,
April 5, 1777, *ibid.*, pp. 38–39; and the proposed letters to Washington and Hancock,
ibid., pp. 39–40; Duc d'Ayen to Gérard, April 11, 1777, A.A.E., Corr. Pol., E.-U., II,
177; Lupton to [Eden], April 8, 1777, Stevens, VII, no. 681.

sphere; yet such pious wishes were valueless as long as Britannia ruled the waves unrivaled, and France hesitated to challenge her control. Where the French government had feared to tread, Lafayette had rushed in. He had defied the mistress of the seas in a little merchant vessel armed with two guns. If an English man-of-war were to meet him, he would undoubtedly repent his foolhardiness. For some of the English were resentful about the French volunteers. When Lafayette's ultimate success was reported in England, an English newspaper printed a "prescription for the cure of Frenchmen suffering from the American malady," which proposed "hanging out of hand every foreign rebel taken armed under the standard of the rebellion."[8]

Despite the real danger incurred by the adolescent sufferer from the "American malady," one minister of France remained calm, almost cynical, throughout the gale of excitement that the youthful daring occasioned. This was Vergennes, secretary of state for foreign affairs. Perhaps he had already made a shrewd guess as to what the outcome would be. In any case he had no objection to heaping coals of fire on Britannia's head, having since the preceding summer consistently followed a policy that was calculated to bring war between the two countries whenever public opinion should overcome the hesitancy of his colleagues. When it was learned in Paris that Lafayette had eluded the king's orders sent to Bordeaux, Vergennes was not in the least discountenanced. He confided to one of the ambassadors at Versailles—probably the Prussian representative, Baron de Goltz,[9] knowing full well that his remarks would be repeated to Lord Stormont—that if the English did use the young scapegrace rather roughly it would be treating him only as his folly deserved. It was, the wily minister said, "such unaccountable folly as there was no foreseeing, no guarding against." But it was a folly common to the young men of France. Many young officers, he admitted, came to consult him about going to

<hr />

[8] "Extrait des papiers anglois du 29 août 1777," A.M.G., carton XLV (Broglie), *chemise* marked "1777, Allemagne, Amérique, Angleterre, Holland, etc.," pièce 9.

[9] Cf. Stormont to Weymouth, April 2, 1777, P.R.O., S.P., France 78/302, no. 58, with Goltz to Frederick, Preussisches Geheimes Staatsarchiv, Rep. XI, Frankreich 89, fasc. 250, fol. 81.

America. "They may, to be sure, do as they please," he concluded, "but . . . . if they come to ask my advice, I give it strongly against their going. If they ask my orders, I forbid them."[10]

When this conversation was reported to Stormont, though he decided that it was too late to see any of the French ministers regarding the episode, he nevertheless considered Vergennes' remarks worthy of being reported to his foreign office. "It would be no difficult matter," the ambassador thought, "to collect M. Vergennes' real sentiment and wishes even from this language, fair and guarded as he thinks it is."[11] Stormont was himself thoroughly convinced of Gallican chicanery. If the English foreign office took the same point of view, Vergennes' tactics might produce the belligerent end he desired sooner than he himself had hoped. Frederick of Prussia contemplated with cynical satisfaction the possibility of a war between his hated enemy France and his distrusted ally England. The enterprise of the Marquis de Lafayette, he thought, would add to the "fermentation."[12]

Nevertheless the English government decided to make no formal protest with regard to Lafayette's escapade. The secrecy with which the young man and his companions had surrounded their enterprise, and particularly his having just been presented to George III ("a step not very consistent with the measures he was then pursuing"), made the English foreign office feel that representations on that subject would be out of order.[13] Stormont therefore bided his time and continued to collect incriminating evidence. He learned that the "brilliant folly of Monsieur de Lafayette" was mentioned in a letter coming from Santo Domingo. Since it took news at least a month to reach America if it traveled rapidly, the ambassador felt that the scheme must have been a long time a-hatching and that it was "very extraordinary" that Lafayette's family and the French

[10] Stormont to Weymouth, April 2, 1777, *loc. cit.*   [11] *Ibid.*

[12] Frederick to Goltz, April 17, 1777, *Politische Correspondenz Friedrich's des Grossen,* XXXIX (Berlin, 1925), 165.

[13] Weymouth to Stormont, April 11, 1777, P.R.O., S.P., France 78/302, no. 24.

ministers should not have known about it.[14] He was also informed that of the fourteen men who were supposed to have accompanied Lafayette, all but a certain lieutenant had received
official leave of absence from Prince Montbarey. This lieutenant wrote to his colonel, seeking to enlist his aid, and Stormont's spies learned of the letter. It was all the more extraordinary, the lieutenant said, that he had not yet received permission to go, since the Comte de Broglie had strongly advised
him to take the step and had promised to solicit Prince Montbarey's interest in his behalf. The colonel, Stormont was informed, had gone to see Prince Montbarey, but received only
an evasive answer: Montbarey "would see what there was to
be done." Stormont had long been suspicious of Broglie's activities. "There is great reason to believe," he now concluded,
"that Comte Broglie secretly encouraged this wild enterprise of
La Fayette."[15]

Broglie was prepared for the finger of suspicion. He and
Deane had been kept informed by frequent letters from Dekalb
of what was happening at Bordeaux. When they found that
there was a general feeling of displeasure in court circles regarding Lafayette's elopement, they quickly took measures to defend themselves. Deane went to see Gérard on the evening of
April 2 and at great length explained his part in the affair, hoping to "satisfy everyone that his conduct has been and would
be strictly honorable."[16] Gérard indeed knew much more about
the Lafayette affair than Deane thought. He, too, was in correspondence with Dekalb, using the same code that the "baron"
employed in writing to St. Paul, chief clerk of the war bureaus,
and also to the Comte de Broglie; and all these men, without
Deane's suspecting it, were aware of one another's interest in
their correspondent.[17]

[14] Stormont to Weymouth, April 9, 1777, *ibid.*, no. 62.

[15] *Ibid.* The lieutenant in question was probably La Colombe, though Lafayette
later assumed responsibility for inducing him to go to America; see Kite, *loc. cit.*, p. 177.

[16] Deane to Gérard, April 2, 1777, *Deane papers*, II, 37.

[17] Dekalb to St. Paul, chef des Bureaux de la Guerre, November 7, 1777, *American
historical review*, XV (1910), 567; Dekalb to Broglie, May 12, [1778], A.A.E., Corr. Pol.,
E.-U., II, 195.

So Deane need not have gone to such great lengths to explain to Gérard his rôle in the conspiracy. The French war office and foreign office already had a very good idea of what was going on, even though they were not so voluble about it as Deane. St. Germain, Vergennes, even Montbarey and Maurepas, had, until the Duc d'Ayen's protests, quietly winked at Broglie's activities. But now that the Noailles family was roused, Gérard had to ask Deane's co-operation in obliging the offending son-in-law to desist. Before the Yankee commissioner left Gérard's quarters, he was intrusted with the packet of letters that the Duc d'Ayen desired sent to Lafayette and had promised to write to Washington and Hancock to inform them that the king of France wished the would-be major-general to return.[18] To shield the French foreign office, the insurgents' agent was made to feel very uncomfortable. Yet, the very next day, when reporting to Vergennes his conversation with Deane, Gérard dismissed the worried American's long-winded explanations with only a few words of casual comment.[19] Deane might have spared himself. The foreign office was not much perturbed about what had happened to Lafayette. Vergennes, when he informed the Marquis de Noailles, Lafayette's uncle in London, of the young man's "caprice," as he called it, said that youthfulness would excuse such behavior; he was himself concerned only because of the feelings of the Marquis de Noailles and the Duc d'Ayen, and the possibility that if Lafayette fell into the hands of the English, he might be treated "with a harshness which is not unknown to that nation."[20]

Upon his return from his interview with Gérard, Deane got into touch with Broglie. Broglie was even better prepared than Deane to defend himself against any charge of undue influence upon Lafayette's actions. He told Deane that he had just received a letter from Lafayette sent from Bordeaux, which cleared him of every possible accusation in that regard. This

[18] Cf. postscript in Deane to Gérard, April 2, 1777, *Deane papers*, II, 37-38; Deane to Vergennes, April 5, 1777, *ibid.*, p. 38, and draft of letters to Washington and Hancock, *ibid.*, pp. 39-40; also *Mémoires*, I, 72.

[19] Gérard to Vergennes, April 3, 1777, A.A.E., Corr. Pol., E.-U., II, 163.

[20] Vergennes to Noailles, April 5, 1777, *ibid.*, Angleterre, DXXII, 353.

letter he was going to communicate to Vergennes. Deane wrote
Gérard about it that same evening, stating that he relied on
Broglie "to explain any and every part of my conduct in this
affair."[21] He also sent along two letters from Dekalb that he
hoped might further justify him. Broglie told several others
about the letter from Lafayette which he depended upon to
prove his innocence, and Stormont soon learned of it. Stormont
did not believe it was authentic, but he secured a copy and sent
it to his government.[22] The letter was allegedly dated at
Bordeaux, March 23. It was to the effect that Broglie had all
along advised Lafayette not to embark upon his venture and
would be surprised to learn that the lad nevertheless had done
so. It concluded with the hope that Broglie would now consent
to aid an enterprise that he no longer could prevent. The appearance of so complete an exoneration for Broglie at just the
opportune moment made Stormont doubt its genuineness. His
guess was only partially right. Actually, though the letter had
been written by Lafayette, it had been prearranged between
Dekalb and his Paris friends.[23] But Stormont could not prove
his suspicions, and no one else was really interested in doing so.
Broglie seemed safe from attack for the time being. He could
afford to feel pleased with himself, for the "Victoire" apparently
was on its way to America with Dekalb and his chosen henchmen.

Meanwhile, in all the hubbub over the escape of the marquis
from Bordeaux, Louis XVI, in his own quiet fashion, had
signed an order forbidding all French officers to take service in
the English colonies without express permission, and instructing
those who had already started out, "and notably M. le Marquis
de Lafayette," to return immediately. This order was the only
measure so far taken which was not directed at Lafayette alone.
If carried out, it would effect a serious step in the direction of
preserving French neutrality in the struggle between the English colonies and their mother-country. Montbarey sent it to

[21] Deane to Gérard, April 2, 1777, *loc. cit.*
[22] Stormont to Weymouth, April 9, 1777, *loc. cit.*
[23] See below, Appen. VIII.

Sartine, the minister of marine and the colonies, to expedite to
the French West Indies, where French boats bound for America
usually called. But Sartine did not share either Maurepas' desire to proceed cautiously in the American crisis or the king's
repugnance to the insurgent colonies. He was more in sympathy with Vergennes' feeling that the wisest tactics for France
to follow would be to support the colonies against the mother-
country until a signal victory on their side and the development
of public opinion in France made open intervention desirable.
Besides, Sartine was a notorious stickler for form. He therefore
sent word to Montbarey (as if he did not have copyists in his
own departmental offices!) that he needed a duplicate and a
triplicate of the king's order so that he might send it out by
three separate vessels "to assure the prompt arrival of one of
the three in the colonies."[24] Nothing further was ever done
about the king's command.

It seemed fairly certain, the first days in April, that Lafayette
would reach America unless the English stopped him. D'Ayen
had already resigned himself to that eventuality. What he
counted on now was to oblige his son-in-law to return almost as
soon as he landed; and the wincing Deane was to be the means
whereby the marquis was thus to be deprived of his victory.
The commissioner had not only promised to send D'Ayen's
packet of letters to America, but also to inform Washington and
Hancock of Louis XVI's wishes. Thus to betray Lafayette and
at the same time to admit his own error was a disagreeable task
for the proud American to perform. He nevertheless prepared
drafts of letters to Washington and Hancock which he submitted to Vergennes for approval. The one to Washington informed him "that [Lafayette's] . . . . going, being without the
approbation or knowledge of the king, is disagreeable and that
His Majesty expects that you will not permit him to take any
command under you." Deane asked the commander-in-chief
to deliver the Duc d'Ayen's letters to the "gallant young hero"
and stated his belief that the defeated lad, despite his disappointment, would respect his king's wishes in the "most ready

[24] Doniol, II, 395, and n. 2.

and agreeable manner." To Hancock Deane wrote more briefly but to the same effect.[25] Deane announced to Vergennes that if these dispatches met with his approval he intended to send them to America within a few days. Once they were sent, everybody but Deane and Lafayette would have won a victory. D'Ayen would be satisfied. Broglie's men would have been brought to America by Lafayette's boat. Vergennes would have roused public discussion of the American question to a fever heat. The English would have been exasperated without being able to prove the complicity of the French government and without having had a proper opportunity for diplomatic protest. But before Vergennes could indicate whether he approved of the dispatches to Washington and Hancock, further developments made the communication of them entirely unnecessary and threatened to rob Broglie and Vergennes of their victory. Just as everyone in Paris had begun to believe the young adventurer on the high seas, well on his way to America, Lafayette returned to Bordeaux.

BIBLIOGRAPHY

The first two volumes of *Deane papers* ("Collections of the New York Historical Society for 1886 and 1887") shed more revealing light upon Deane's activities in connection with the Lafayette episode than the biographers have hitherto allowed to be seen. The correspondence of Deane with Gérard and Vergennes is contained here more completely than in the Archives of the Ministry of Foreign Affairs in Paris, and the additional documents are of prime importance.

Many of the documents here quoted from the archives of the ministry of foreign affairs are also to be found in part in Doniol's volumes and in Stevens' *Facsimiles*. Several of Stormont's dispatches to Weymouth are also to be found in Stevens' *Facsimiles*, and partially in Vol. III of Friedrich von Raumer, *Europa vom Ende des Siebenjahrigen bis zum Ende des amerikanischen Krieges (1763–1783) nach den Quellen in britischen und französischen Reichsarchive* (Leipzig, 1839).

[25] Deane to Vergennes, April 5, 1777 (with two inclosures), *Deane papers*, II, 38–40.

CHAPTER X

Return and Escape Again

THE "Victoire" dropped her anchor behind the rocky island that guards the well-secluded harbor of Los Pasajes in Spain on March 28, 1777. There Lafayette, despite Dekalb's impatience, decided to remain until the return of his courier from Paris with definite news of what his family and the ministry were saying and doing. They did not have to wait that long, however. The leisurely progress of a sailing vessel along the shores of the Bay of Biscay could easily be detected. M. de Fumel, commandant of Bordeaux, had no great difficulty in discovering the destination of the "Victoire" and had dispatched a courier with the king's orders to San Sebastian. He arrived on March 31, bringing the court's command that the marquis go to Marseilles to join the Duc d'Ayen and the Comtesse de Tessé for a tour of Italy.[1]

The beautiful plan to go off to America at the marquis' expense now seemed to Dekalb to be completely frustrated because of the lad's unwillingness either to do as his family wished or to defy them entirely by doing as he himself liked. "His course was silly from the moment he could not make up his mind quietly to execute his project, undisturbed by threats," the exasperated "baron" wrote to his wife. "Had he told me in Paris all that he has admitted since, I would have remonstrated most earnestly against the whole scheme." Yet, despite his chagrin, he let fall a note of admiration for the boy's behavior. "If it be said that he has done a foolish thing, it may be an-

[1] Dekalb to Mme Dekalb, April 1, 1777, Kapp, p. 104, and Colleville, p. 130; see also Appen. VII. The order, while issued, as was customary, in the king's name, was probably the actual work of Maurepas.

swered that he acted from the most honorable motives, and that he can hold up his head before all high-minded men."[2] Vacillating between his sympathy for the marquis and his anxiety to get to the field of action before the spring campaign was over, Dekalb advised his companion to go back to Bordeaux, make some arrangement with Basmarein and Raimbaux for the return of the "Victoire," and then proceed to Marseilles. He argued that if Lafayette could induce the shipowners to release him from his contract by keeping 20,000 or 25,000 livres out of the 40,000 already paid them, the improvident marquis would recover at least part of his futile investment and be well out of the affair. Secretly, Dekalb hoped that he could himself then drive a good bargain with the Bordeaux shippers.[3]

The younger man clung stubbornly, however, to his intention to sail for America. He still felt that his family's interference with this splendid opportunity must be due to some misunderstanding. He would go to Bordeaux and try to learn more exactly what the court wished. He would send home more letters and entreaties. If necessary he would himself go to Paris or even to Marseilles to see his father-in-law. Dekalb must not sail without him unless he received definite orders to that effect. Dekalb promised. After all, it was still the boy's boat! The two men went off to dinner at San Sebastian, and immediately afterward Lafayette started for Bordeaux. It was April 1—the very moment when in Paris everyone was excitedly gossiping about the "Victoire's" escape from the southern seaport. "Time will hang heavy on my hands here in the meantime," wrote the discouraged "baron" to his faithful spouse. "I do not believe he will be able to rejoin me. . . . . This is the end of his expedition to America to join the army of the insurgents."[4] Dekalb soon started negotiations through his wife with Basmarein in Paris, offering him 24,000 livres if he would take back the "Victoire" and send her off on his own account. Basmarein refused to

<hr/>

[2] April 6–7, 1777, Kapp, pp. 105–6.

[3] Castex, "Pierre de Basmarein," *Revue des questions historiques*, CII (1925), 106.

[4] April 1, 1777, Kapp, pp. 104–5; Colleville, pp. 129–32; I have changed the order of the sentences in this quotation.

agree to such a bargain. Dekalb also thought of leaving San Sebastian and going to Paris or the Île de Ré or Nantes to wait for a boat that Deane might provide.[5] But he soon learned that he had underestimated his young friend's pertinacity and that it would be wise to wait in Spain for further developments.

It took three days to go by post from San Sebastian to Bordeaux past St. Jean-de-Luz and Bayonne. At St. Jean-de-Luz the uneasy boy exchanged a few words with the post-master's daughter. Otherwise it was a lonely trip and the disappointed major-general had plenty of time to meditate upon the wrongs done to him. This was the first thing he had really wanted to do since, as a child, he had hoped to encounter the hyena of Gévaudan and kill it with his bare hands. Almost everything else he had attempted since then had been determined by an old-maid aunt or a senescent great-grandfather or a sarcastic father-in-law, unless, as in more trivial affairs, it had been prescribed by an adolescent desire to emulate the admired Vicomte de Noailles. Here, for once, his wealth seemed to enable him to do that which even the Vicomte de Noailles could not do—something that he had, vaguely at first, more keenly afterward, dreamed of doing since the famous dinner at Metz in honor of the Duke of Gloucester. Until the very last minute, despite the Duc d'Ayen's contempt, he had believed that if he could only get enough credit out of it, such as an appointment to a major-general's rank, even the Duc d'Ayen would take him seriously and allow him to seek for glory in America. Then, if France went to war with England, as she probably would, or if his family affairs called him back, he could return as a success, with dignity and prestige assured. Mme de Hunolstein would no longer be indifferent to him and the courtiers of the queen would no longer dare to laugh at his performance in a quadrille. But now, if he yielded, there would be nothing left for him to do except to trail after an old lady and two old gentlemen in Italy. If he refused to go, there might be a prison sentence for him by *lettre de cachet*. His friends must already be sneering at him. Dekalb quite obviously had thought he was a blundering fool.

[5] Castex, *loc. cit.;* and Dekalb to Mme Dekalb, April 6, Kapp, pp. 106–7.

Deane must be exceedingly annoyed to learn that his zealous protégé had been mistaken in leading the Americans to believe that the Duc d'Ayen would raise no difficulties if he were made a major-general. His overanxious sacrifice seemed likely to result only in great embarrassment to the American cause, which he so much wished to aid.[6] Somehow everything he tried to do seemed doomed to failure. Still if only he could now persuade the Duc d'Ayen to change his mind, they would all yet be proud to know him and to call him friend.

Arrived in Bordeaux (April 3), Lafayette went immediately to see M. de Fumel, the commandant of the port. He told that gentleman that he alone was responsible for what had happened and was ready to face the consequences. He begged Fumel's permission to go to Paris, pleading for two weeks in which to see his wife and family.[7] Fumel refused. He must go to Marseilles as the court had ordered, and wait until the tour of Italy should begin. He must be there on the fifteenth. The disconsolate lad sent off a courier to Maurepas in the hope of obtaining a revocation of the order, and also addressed a brief letter to Carmichael apologizing that his "good will should have so little success." "Force," he said, "may prevent me from rendering you the service I should like, but as it has no effect upon hearts, I shall not be prevented from remaining all my life your brother and your friend."[8]

The letters that the marquis' courier brought to Paris created an erroneous impression there. Maurepas believed that the message which he received from the offending lad in Bordeaux ended the matter. He told Stormont that it was "a letter of excuse" in which the youthful transgressor gave his "formal submission."[9] Vergennes also thought that Lafayette had "submitted to the king's orders."[10] They little knew the doggedness of the

[6] Cf. Dekalb to Deane, April 17, 1777, *Deane papers*, II, 49.

[7] Lafayette to Mme Lafayette, April 9, 1777, in the collection of M. Emmanuel Fabius, of Paris (see p. 15 above); Dekalb to Mme Dekalb, April 12, 1777, Kapp, p. 107.

[8] Lafayette to Carmichael, [April, 1777], L.C., House of Rep. papers, no. 97.

[9] Stormont to Weymouth, April 29, 1777, P.R.O., S.P., France 78/302, no. 81.

[10] Vergennes to the Marquis de Noailles, April 11, 1777, A.A.E., Corr. Pol., Angleterre, DXXII, 399 v.

timid lad. His letters were so cautiously worded as to give the impression that he was willing to surrender, though actually he did not yet consider himself beaten. But when his courier returned from Paris, he was quite convinced that the court would not relent. Because his mailpouch contained no communication from Maurepas, the discouraged boy assumed that the minister did not even deign to reply to a request he considered so indiscreet.[11] On April 12 the despairing lad decided to go to Marseilles, where he was required to be within three days, and there try to persuade the Duc d'Ayen to give him the consent that he had so far failed to win. It was his last card, but the tone in which he wrote Dekalb begging the old soldier to continue to stand by was still hopeful. Dekalb, however, was disgusted. "If I am to wait until he gets to Marseilles, I shall have to remain here until the 26th," he protested.[12]

Meanwhile, at Paris the unexpected return of the prodigal marquis had been bruited abroad. Deane learned on April 7 that the young Frenchman had returned to Bordeaux and immediately wrote to Gérard to find out what to do with the dispatches he had been asked to send to Lafayette in America.[13] Though Deane was somewhat relieved to find that he would not now have publicly to avow his error in assuming there would be no protest to his recruiting of Lafayette, Carmichael was completely disgusted and planned to return home.[14] Stormont discovered the new turn of affairs only on April 9. He exulted that "Lafayette's expedition has been a short one indeed."[15] He was even led to believe that Lafayette had been temporarily imprisoned in the Château Trompette at Bordeaux.[16] On April 11, Vergennes, writing to inform the Marquis de Noailles that

[11] *Mémoires*, I, 69–70.

[12] Dekalb to Mme Dekalb, April 15, 1777, Kapp, p. 107.

[13] Deane to Gérard, April 8, 1777, A.A.E., Corr. Pol., E.-U., II, 173; *Deane papers*, II, 43.

[14] Carmichael to Dumas, April 21, 1777, *Deane papers*, II, 49.

[15] Stormont to Weymouth, April 9, 1777, P.R.O., S.P., France 78/302, no. 62.

[16] *Ibid.*, no. 70 (April 16); and *Espion anglais*, VI, 69 (under date of May 26, 1777).

"very happily" Lafayette had come back and would accompany the Duc d'Ayen to Italy, congratulated the ambassador on having avoided the embarrassment of seeing his nephew in the ranks of the insurgents.[17] Maurepas likewise wrote Noailles that "by the merest chance" the Marquis de Lafayette's "beautiful project" had been arrested.[18] The French ambassador was greatly relieved. He had only recently had a conversation with Lord Suffolk, of the British foreign office, in which that gentleman had let drop a remark that "the winds had been very good for several days for trade between England and America." The sensitive envoy wondered whether this was not a subtle reference "to the departure for the American army of a person close to me."[19]

No one felt more relieved than the Duc d'Ayen and his family at Gilbert's apparent change of heart. Much gratified by his son-in-law's return, the Duc d'Ayen asked Gérard to get back the packet of letters which was to have been forwarded to Lafayette. His public attitude toward his errant ward now changed so completely that Stormont erroneously believed him to have entered into collusion with Lafayette to outwit his government.[20] Together with his sister and her husband, D'Ayen soon set out for Marseilles, where he expected to find a chastened Lafayette and begin the directed tour of Italy.

It was, however, the Comte de Broglie who was principally responsible for Lafayette's next decisive step. That wily aristocrat had kept in fairly close touch with the ministers of France. Both Vergennes and Maurepas knew of his plans and had done nothing to check them. Maurepas, fearful of embarrassing entanglements, probably would have liked to do so, but lacked the vigor to proceed actively against so powerful a figure. Vergennes, though he was apprehensive of Broglie's political influence and afraid that his intrigues might yet destroy the minis-

[17] Vergennes to Noailles, April 11, 1777, *loc. cit.*

[18] Maurepas to Noailles, April 15, 1777, *ibid.*, fol. 408.

[19] Doniol, II, 399; cf. Vergennes to Noailles, April 19, 1777, A.A.E., Corr. Pol., Angleterre, DXXII, 340 v.

[20] Stormont to Weymouth, May 7, 1777, P.R.O., S.P., France 78/302, no. 82.

try, felt that the comte's American ambitions might be useful in creating the Franco-American alliance which he was himself so earnestly engaged in promoting.[21] Consequently Broglie found it no difficult matter to discover what was the government's real attitude toward the vacillating marquis at Bordeaux. He soon satisfied himself that the ministers were acting only out of respect for the wishes of the Noailles family, that even the royal order would not have been issued but for the complaints of the Duc d'Ayen, that in reality neither the king nor anybody else was angry with the lad for "so noble an enterprise."[22]

Broglie had been careful to appear innocent as long as it was believed that Lafayette was on his way to America taking with him Dekalb and his other henchmen. The unexpected return of the blundering lad to Bordeaux suddenly destroyed Broglie's self-satisfaction. If the hesitant young man were not to start off again soon, the whole expedition might fail as had the previous one at Le Havre, and Broglie, along with Lafayette, might himself become the laughingstock of the nation.[23] Lafayette must be informed that the situation was not so critical as it seemed. Broglie decided to send the Vicomte de Mauroy to persuade the young man to continue with his original plans. Mauroy was, next to Dekalb, the man most enthusiastically indorsed by Broglie. He had been engaged by Deane as major-general to go with Dekalb the preceding December but had not been included among those who were to sail on the "Victoire."[24] He was now dispatched to Bordeaux to join Lafayette and to pro-

[21] Stormont to Weymouth, April 16, 1777, *ibid.*, no. 69; *idem* to *idem*, May 7, 1777, *ibid.*, no. 82.

[22] Dekalb to Deane, April 17, 1777, *Deane papers*, II, 47; Dekalb to Mme DeKalb, April 17, 1777, Kapp, pp. 107-8. Dekalb could have learned this only from Mauroy (see below, p. 120) or from Lafayette, who had learned it from Mauroy; and Mauroy had come almost immediately from Broglie. Dekalb's actual words to his wife are that "the ministers, being asked their real sentiments in the matter," replied as indicated in the above text. In view of what must have been the ultimate source of Dekalb's information, it is not difficult to guess who asked the ministers. Cf. Bacourt, I, 66-67; and Lameth, pp. 106-7. We know from Deane's letter to Gérard of April 2, 1777 (*Deane papers*, II, 37), that Broglie kept in touch with Vergennes during this period.

[23] Bacourt, I, 67.

[24] See contract of Mauroy, November 20, 1776, *Deane papers*, I, 359-60; cf. Stevens, III, nos. 251 and 254.

ceed with the hesitating youth to America. Armed with a personal letter from Broglie to Washington, and another from Deane to the president of Congress, Mauroy started out from Paris on April 8. He had been fully informed of what to say to Lafayette not only by Broglie but also by Carmichael.[25]

When Mauroy reached Bordeaux, he was almost too late. Lafayette had already secured from M. de Fumel a passport permitting him to go to Marseilles and was on the point of departure. Mauroy easily gave Lafayette to understand that all of the hullabaloo had been raised only to please the Noailles family and that everybody else thought the enterprise noble and generous. The ministers had more or less reluctantly been "made to take"[26] the part of disapproving his conduct by the tempest which the Duc d'Ayen had raised. But if Lafayette would return to Spain and sail, no serious consequences would follow for him.

This was exhilarating news indeed for the crestfallen youth. Despair suddenly changed to elation. He sat himself down and wrote a hasty letter to Maurepas. Since the minister had not replied to his previous letter, he said, he assumed that silence meant approval and would act accordingly. Then, dispatching the letter, he started out for the Spanish border. His passport, however, was issued for Marseilles. In order to avoid suspicion and detection, he left Bordeaux by the Marseilles coach, in which Mauroy was also a passenger. When they had gone a sufficient distance from the city, they left the carriage. Despite Mauroy's assurances that the government really did not wish to stop him, Lafayette was disturbed by the rumor, which Mauroy had also brought, that orders to arrest him had been sent out by vessel. Refusing, therefore, to take any chances, he disguised himself as a courier and, reversing his direction, took the road that went past Bayonne into Spain. He galloped all the way ahead

[25] Deane to the president of Congress, April 8, 1777, Wharton, II, 304–5; Lafayette to Carmichael, April 19, 1777, L.C., House of Rep. papers, no. 99. Deane's letter speaks of Viscount Mourreu, but the context makes it perfectly clear that it is Mauroy who is meant. For Broglie's letter to Washington, April 8, 1777, see Kite, "Lafayette and his companions on the 'Victoire' " (continued), *loc. cit.*, p. 159.

[26] The phrase is Lafayette's; Lafayette to Maurepas, A.A.E., Corr. Pol. E.-U., II, 250–58; (published also in *Mémoires*, I, 108, where it is erroneously said to be addressed to Vergennes).

of the carriage which Mauroy occupied, procuring relays at the posthouses and discharging the other duties of an outrider. When they came to Bayonne, he hid in the stable while Mauroy tended to some errands. At St. Jean-de-Luz, he was badly frightened because the postman's daughter, to whom he had spoken on the way to Bordeaux, recognized him through his disguise. He signaled her not to reveal his identity and he felt she understood. There was really nothing to cause the slightest apprehension. There were no pursuers. M. de Fumel had been led to believe that Lafayette had started out toward Marseilles, and no one else was in a position to order pursuit. In fact, it was known that he had not gone to Marseilles, as he had promised, only when he failed to arrive there at the appointed time.[27] Yet the excited lad was sure that he owed his escape to this young heroine of the St. Jean-de-Luz posthouse. There must have been soldiers sent out to capture him! Since they never caught up with him, it could have been only because the postman's daughter deliberately misdirected them. Though he did not wait to find out whether this actually was the true explanation, and never saw the young lady again, ever afterward Lafayette remained grateful to her for her "adroit loyalty."[28]

While waiting for Lafayette, Dekalb had moored the "Victoire" in the secluded harbor at Los Pasajes, close by San Sebastian, where he believed she would be quite secure.[29] On April 17 the baron and his fellow-officers were delighted to see Lafayette and Mauroy galloping toward them. Dekalb immediately hastened to share the good news with his wife, Broglie, and Deane.[30] It was obvious that the "Victoire's" passengers must now make haste lest, before they sailed, they should learn of another change of mind on the part of the French government. All was made ready within three days.

On the eve of their departure Lafayette sent a half-defiant,

[27] Cf. Stormont to Weymouth, April 29, 1777, P.R.O., S.P., France 78/302, no. 81.

[28] Lafayette, *Mémoires*, I, 14–15, 69–70; Sparks, V, 449, and Ducoudray-Holstein, *Mémoires of Lafayette*, (2d ed., 1835), p. 33, are identical and must be used very critically.

[29] See Appen. VII below.

[30] Kapp, p. 107; Stormont to Weymouth, May 7, 1777, P.R.O., S.P., France 78/302, no. 82; *Deane papers*, II, 47–48.

half-imploring letter to Adrienne. They had tried to frighten him into obedience, he told her; they would have found that persuasion would have succeeded better. But she was not to worry about him. He was taking this trip more as a philosopher than as a soldier and would be in no great danger. He might even return from America sooner than the Duc d'Ayen from Italy. He loved her very much, he said, and begged her to forgive him and to take good care of Henriette and their "other child."[31]

He also wrote to Carmichael "the last letter that you will receive from me in French." It had been the fear of hurting his friends somehow or other, he said, that had made him ready to sacrifice his desire to go to America. Now that such a sacrifice had proved unnecessary, he would not lose an instant and would sail "full of joy, hope and zeal for our common cause." He could not resist the temptation to congratulate himself a little. "I have been told that Milord Stormont was somewhat displeased with my behavior. Altogether this affair has produced the éclat that I desired, and at this moment everybody has his eyes on us. I will try to justify this celebrity. I assume responsibility for not being captured by the English, and I hope that you will feel re-assured. . . . . The only favor that I wish is that I be afforded every possible opportunity to use my fortune, my labors, all the resources of my imagination and to shed my blood for my brothers and my friends. The only reward that I shall ask after I succeed is to find some new way to be useful to them." Very confident, now that he was once more out of France, that all would go well, he felt it his turn to reassure Carmichael. "You may feel entirely at ease as far as my family is concerned, and even about that order that I received. Once I am gone, everybody will be of my opinion. Once I have conquered, everybody will applaud my enterprise."[32]

Thus, on Sunday, April 20, 1777, carrying with her a boy whose emotions were a sad mixture of triumph and defiance,

---

[31] Lafayette to Mme Lafayette, April 19, 1777 (copy in hand of Mme Lafayette), collection of M. Emmanuel Fabius (see p. 15 above).

[32] Lafayette to Carmichael, April 19, 1777, L.C., House of Rep. papers, no. 99; see also below, Appen. IX.

sorrow at leaving his old friends, devotion to his new, and eagerness for a full and brilliant career ("I hope," he had written to Carmichael, "that I will prove as good a general as I am a good American"), the "Victoire" sailed out of the rocky gorge that forms the harbor of Los Pasajes and soon began to lose the foothills of the Pyrenees in the distance.

BIBLIOGRAPHY

Lafayette's *Mémoires* contain two separate accounts of his escape. The first of these (I, 13–15) was written shortly after the War of Independence, probably in 1783 or 1784, and is the more reliable. It is necessarily, however, a description of what he alone saw and thought, which was not all that was to be seen and thought. This account must be supplemented, not only by the second version contained in the *Mémoires* (I, 68–71, written sometime during the Napoleonic Consulate), but also by Lafayette's contemporary letters and by those of Dekalb, contained in Kapp's biography, and of Deane, contained in the *Deane papers*. When this is done, it will be seen that the narrative of the escape given by Sparks (*Writings of George Washington*, V, Appen. I), which is the source most often exploited by Lafayette's biographers in this connection, is thoroughly unreliable. Whether it was manufactured by Sparks himself—a possibility which is enhanced by Sparks's well-known lack of scruple in this regard (cf. Smyth, *Writings of Benjamin Franklin*, I, 30–32)— or whether he only reproduced in printed form a version dictated by his hero (see above, p. 82), it contains many unplausible details that in Lafayette's last years had already become part of the Lafayette legend. It is no more than possible, for instance, that the marquis could have argued with Maurepas that the permission given to a French officer (named Banklay) to volunteer in the English army was a good reason for his being allowed to volunteer in the American, since Banklay's action was not generally known until some time later (cf. Doniol, II, 399), though it was already reported by the *nouvellistes* in March and April (cf. *Correspondance secrète inédite sur Louis XVI*, I, 34 and 43; *Journal de Métra*, IV, 265; and the *New England palladium*, July 6, 1824, quoting a Paris account dated April 4, 1777). It sounds much more fictitious that Lafayette should at this time have taunted Maurepas with the, to say the least, discourteous remark in a letter he is supposed to have sent to his family that "when the ministers should be faithful to their pledges to the people, they might with a better grace talk about [Lafayette's] violation of an oath to the government." This is an effort to attribute to the young aristocrat democratic notions which in 1777 he did not yet have and an irreverence of which at that time he would hardly have been guilty. Lafayette's prior account (*Mémoires*, I, 14) does not give these two probably anachronistic details. Nevertheless, because, in any case, Lafayette co-operated with Sparks in the production of this appendix, the latter's story contains some information not available elsewhere and, if checked with the utmost caution, can be made to yield some details of great interest.

CHAPTER XI

Approbation

O N APRIL 20, 1777, at almost the very moment the "Victoire" lifted anchor and sailed away from the Spanish coast, Mme du Deffand sat herself down to inform Horace Walpole that Lafayette had been caught at San Sebastian and would leave for Italy with the Duc d'Ayen.[1] It was not until the letters of Dekalb and Lafayette, written on the eve of departure, reached Paris that his friends realized that he had not gone to Marseilles but had returned to Spain. Carmichael, quite naturally, knew about this before any other (April 24) and told George Lupton, who immediately informed the British government.[2] Dr. Edward Bancroft also learned of it on the same day and probably from the same source.[3] There was very little that took place at the Hôtel d'Hambourg which the English did not soon discover through one channel or another.

When the news of the marquis' latest step was brought to the Noailles hôtel, the Duc d'Ayen, accompanied by his sister and his brother-in-law, had already arrived at Marseilles (April 21)[4] and found no Lafayette. The erratic youth was by that time well upon the high seas. In the Duc d'Ayen's absence from Paris, his father, the Marshal de Noailles, went to see Maurepas in order to express the family's displeasure and affliction. Maurepas reassured him, and also hastened to calm any apprehensions that Lafayette's uncle, the French ambassador in Lon-

---

[1] Du Deffand, pp. 602–3; Walpole already knew it, however: cf. *Last journal of Horace Walpole*, II, 20 (under date of April 15, 1777).

[2] [Lupton] to [Eden], April 24, 1777, Stevens, VII, no. 686.

[3] B[ancroft] to W[entworth], April 24, 1777, *ibid.*, I, no. 65.

[4] *Gazette de Leyde*, May 16, 1777.

don, might have. The members of the Noailles family had no
reason to feel guilty, the minister wrote; the king could not hold
any of them responsible for "the actions of a young man whose
head has been turned."[5] Vergennes was likewise uneasy about
the possible effect of Lafayette's "effervescence" on the Marquis
de Noailles, but coolly waited to inform him about his nephew's
latest escapade until the envoy had learned of it from other
sources. While declaring Lafayette's advisers to be "altogether
blameworthy," Vergennes made it quite obvious that he was
not really disturbed by what had happened. "I do not know,"
he announced to the Marquis de Noailles, after Lafayette was
already almost two weeks at sea, "whether the king is aware of
this second caprice; I shall take good care not to speak to him
about it."[6] The ambassador could have had no difficulty in understanding that Vergennes would take no serious measures
regarding his young relation's maneuvers.

Though the foreign office in London had already heard from
persons close to Deane and Carmichael of Lafayette's final
escape, Stormont's own informers were not so thorough as usual
on this occasion. It was only on April 28 in an interview with
Maurepas that Stormont learned of it. With some embarrassment, the French minister, believing it better that he tell the
English ambassador than that Stormont learn it from others,
mentioned that Lafayette had again gone "to prosecute his wild
enterprise." Up to this time Stormont had avoided speaking
directly to the French government upon the Lafayette affair,
but since Maurepas had himself opened the subject, Stormont
now talked quite freely. This new development, he declared,
was the consequence of His Excellency's having taken only half-
measures. "It would not have happened if instead of stopping
Lafayette alone, the ship and all the officers on board had been
required to return to France."[7] A little later on the same day
Stormont also went to see Vergennes. That worthy adopted the

[5] Maurepas to the Marquis de Noailles, April 28, 1777, A.A.E., Corr. Pol., Angleterre, DXXII, 502.

[6] Vergennes to the Marquis de Noailles, May 2, 1777, Doniol, II, 411.

[7] Stormont to Weymouth, April 29, 1777, P.R.O., S.P., France 78/302, no. 81.

same subterfuge he had previously found advantageous—expatiating upon the young adventurer's folly. He likewise lamented the large sums of money the young man was said to have drawn in favor of the insurgents. When the British envoy again brought up the lack of any effort on the part of the French government to retain the officers who accompanied Lafayette, Vergennes "answered, as he always does upon these subjects, like a man who knows he is upon bad ground and wishes to get off by evasion."[8] Stormont derived no satisfaction from this interview. Vergennes persisted in pretending that the episode had no real importance. "Lord Stormont," he afterward wrote to the Marquis de Noailles, "is in very bad humor about it. He has a talent for assigning great importance to very petty things."[9]

At the time that these interviews took place the French ministers had at their disposal only the information that the Marshal de Noailles had provided, and Stormont knew even less than they. When he had acquired more complete and exact details of what had happened, the ambassador returned to see Maurepas (May 5). He again insisted that Lafayette's "extravagant project" might have been prevented "by proper steadiness." "It was astonishing," he protested, "that the vessel should have been suffered to proceed on her voyage." Maurepas, a little uneasy, tried to change the subject by resorting to witticism. He facetiously described how the ladies of Paris railed at Lafayette's father-in-law for trying to stop "so noble and spirited an enterprise." Pleasantry, reported the exasperated Stormont, is Maurepas' "usual way of getting off disagreeable ground."[10]

Finding he could still get no satisfaction out of Maurepas, Stormont went once more to see Vergennes. The foreign secretary likewise tried to avoid responsibility by the familiar practice of blaming someone else. He attacked Broglie, calling him "a great busy-body," one of those at Paris "who make ministers." Stormont replied that the ministers of Versailles might

[8] Ibid.   [9] Vergennes to the Marquis de Noailles, May 2, 1777, Doniol, II, 411.
[10] Stormont to Weymouth, May 7, 1777, P.R.O., S.P., France 78/302, no. 82.

be the only ones if they pleased. Vergennes agreed and asked
Stormont to express this opinion to Maurepas. "I am far from
believing," Stormont wrote to Weymouth, "that M. de Vergennes wishes M. Maurepas to act a fair uniform part with
regard to the rebels, but I am persuaded he laments his unsteadiness that leaves room for others to interfere and sees the advantage such unsteadiness gives to those busy, turbulent spirits
who are anxious for a change of ministry, in which change M.
de Vergennes would of course find himself involved."[11] Before
taking leave of Vergennes, Stormont declared that the ship
carrying Lafayette had no right to the protection of the French
colors, and, should she fall into British hands, must be considered as belonging to the enemy. Vergennes only shrugged his
shoulders and made no direct reply.[12]

The Noailles family once more was left to its grief and chagrin.
Somehow they felt that their prestige and reputation for family
cohesion had suffered greatly because of Gilbert's recklessness.
The thirtieth of April was to have been a joyous day in the
Noailles household. On that date Adrienne's aunt, the youngest
sister of the Duchesse d'Ayen, married the Comte de Ségur,
the best of Gilbert's friends, if the Vicomte de Noailles be ex-
cepted. By that ceremony Ségur became his comrade's uncle.
But the friend and nephew was not among those present. Indeed, he was even responsible for the absence of the bride's
brother-in-law who had hastened off to join him at Marseilles.
Adrienne heard reproaches directed against her husband on all
sides, but hid her own tears lest she appear afflicted and add to
her family's mortification.[13]

The letter which Gilbert had sent Adrienne on the eve of his
departure from Los Pasajes was the last word that they were to
receive from him until the beginning of August.[14] Vague rumors
of his exploits soon reached them. Late in May it was reported
that Lafayette had landed at Boston or Portsmouth with four

[11] *Ibid.*   [12] *Ibid.*, no. 84.

[13] *Journal de Paris*, no. 122, May 2, 1777, p. 4; Lafayette to Latour-Maubourg,
January, 1808, Lasteyrie, pp. 432–33.

[14] "Notice sur Mme. d'Ayen," *loc. cit.*, p. 59.

thousand French soldiers.[15] This impossible tale was regarded
as confirmed when, in July, an American vessel came to Bordeaux carrying the news that the young hero had disembarked—
this time at Providence—amid a burst of popular enthusiasm
that enabled him immediately to raise a corps of 300,000 men.
The Mouchy family—particularly the Prince de Poix—were
said to be beside themselves with joy.[16]

Adrienne did not allow herself to become the victim of these
false illusions. The failing health of her daughter, Henriette, the
illness of other relatives, and her own great need to reserve her
strength against the birth of her expected child kept her preoccupied. The departure of the Polish Count Pulaski, who
started out from Paris in May to join the American insurgents,
gave her a chance to communicate once more with Gilbert.[17]
Shortly afterward (July 1) her second baby—another girl—was
born and christened Anastasie-Louise-Pauline. Lafayette was
to learn of this only in December, and by that time his older
daughter, Henriette, had died.

Despite her determination to suffer in silence, Adrienne sometimes wept and became reproachful when she encountered her
husband's friends. Deane did what he could to reassure her
family, but the three months without word from the beloved adventurer who had embarked upon unknown seas in a frail
vessel were filled with lively fears. Notwithstanding his assurances that he would take care of himself, they were worried
that he might take unnecessary risks.

They were also afraid that he might not have enough money,
especially after they heard that some misunderstanding about
his contract with Basmarein would prevent his using his share
of the profit to be derived from the sale of the cargo carried on
the "Victoire." They immediately sent him five hundred

---

[15] Lescure (ed.), *Correspondance secrète inédite sur Louis XVI, etc.*, I, 60–61 (under
date of May 26, 1777); the identical report is given also in *Correspondance de Métra*, IV,
384; cf. Stormont to Weymouth, July 16, 1777, P.R.O., S.P., France 78/303, no. 117.

[16] Unknown writer to Basmarein, July 5, 1777, contained in letter of Lupton to
Eden, July 15, 1777, Stevens, III, no. 257.

[17] Mme Lafayette to [Pulaski] May 27, [1777] in the Jackson Collection, Yale University Library; Lafayette to Mme Lafayette, October 1, 1777, *Mémoires*, I, 104.

pounds sterling. They sent no more only because they had no
confidence in his ability to take care of his resources, and realized how easily his friends could impose upon his generosity.
Since his departure for England he had lavished money so freely
that his steward could not keep up with the demands made
upon him. Before the end of the year 1777 Lafayette was to
spend nearly $170,000 (138,433 livres) in cash and to accumu-
late over $200,000 (168,327 livres) in short-term debts.[18] It was
quite obvious that a youth still in his teens who knew so little
about the meaning of wealth ought not to be intrusted with
large sums. Yet his family feared to leave him penniless in a
foreign country, and finally some of them went to see the
American agents about it. Franklin decided to put the matter
before Washington, requesting the American commander-in-
chief to advance whatever sums Lafayette might need against
the marquis' draft, which the Noailles family would then honor.
Franklin also begged Washington to favor the youthful Frenchman with his counsel, assuring the general that this would be
"an act of benevolence gratefully remembered and acknowl-
edged by a number of worthy persons in France who interest
themselves extremely in the welfare of the amiable young
nobleman."[19] At about the same time Franklin and Deane
wrote to the American Committee of Foreign Affairs, suggest-
ing, for the sake of Lafayette's "beautiful young wife," that
Washington curb the young man's "bravery and ardent desire
to distinguish himself" so as to avoid "his being hazarded
much." "He is exceedingly beloved," they added, "and everybody's good wishes attend . . . . his expedition. . . . . Those
who censure it as imprudent of him, do nevertheless applaud his
spirit."[20]

With this official dispatch Deane inclosed a personal letter
to Robert Morris of the Committee. He begged Morris to act

[18] Gerard to Mlle du Motier, December 27, 1777, University of Chicago Library,
DC 146, f. L2 A3, Vol. I.

[19] Smyth, *Writings of Benjamin Franklin*, VII, 61–62; Smyth believed that this letter
was written in August, 1777, but, as the writer did not yet know whether Lafayette
had already seen Washington, it was probably written earlier.

[20] May 25, 1777, Wharton, II, 324–25.

"as a father" to the gullible stripling and protect him from adventurers among his own countrymen. At the same moment Deane once more sought to impress upon Congress the advantage to be derived from Lafayette's brilliant connections and the youth's own lack of mercenary motives. "A generous reception of him will do us infinite service. He is above pecuniary considerations. . . . . All he seeks is glory, and every one here says he has taken the most noble method to procure it. You may think it makes a great noise in Europe and at the same time see that well managed it will greatly help us." Deane's satisfaction with the éclat which both he and Lafayette had expected from their conspiracy and had now achieved was evident in the complacent tone in which he wrote. "It has occasioned much conversation here and though the court pretends to know nothing of the matter, his conduct is highly extolled by the first people in France."[21] Apparently Deane's qualms and trepidations on his own account were now at rest, though he still had some misgivings because of the "generous disposition" of the chief puppet in his little comedy. On that score he was not mistaken, but it was not Lafayette's countrymen who were to consume the greater part of the fortune that this generosity determined the young man to spend within the next few years.

The secret precautions which the Noailles family now took for their lad's comfort and safety revealed quite a different attitude from that of the cynical Duc d'Ayen. Since the duke was away in Italy and everybody else approved, the Noailles family had begun to look with increasing favor, though with none too great confidence, upon the wayward son-in-law. Upon returning from his journey D'Ayen found his disobedient ward a popular hero. No less a notable than the illustrious Voltaire soon gave the young adventurer his stamp of approval. At the Duc de Choiseul's house, one day during his fatal triumphal sojourn in Paris, the Sage of Ferney singled out from a numerous assemblage of admirers the Marquise de Lafayette. Falling on his knees before her, he gallantly expressed his admiration of

---

[21] Deane to Robert Morris, May 26, 1777, L.C., papers of the Continental Congress, Acquisition 2827.

her noble husband. The old man's posturing brought both embarrassment and joy to the modest Adrienne.[22] Her mingled feelings would have been even more acute had she known that besides Voltaire, Franklin, Mme du Deffand, and Horace Walpole other literary celebrities were equally interested in Gilbert's exploits; that the historian Gibbon had for a time found him the chief topic of conversation in London society;[23] and that Franklin, in order to announce to his friends in England the young man's achievement, had chosen no less a messenger than the Abbé Raynal.[24] Far from the *philosophes'* having influenced the young aristocrat to embark upon his course, the truth seemed to be that they were now being influenced by him. The spectacle of a rich lord, married to a beautiful lady, rushing off to aid embattled farmers to establish the Laws of Nature and of Nature's God in a new world was for them an edifying one indeed, even if their perspective was somewhat warped by wishful thinking. The courtier and landlord still in his teens was well on the way to becoming a symbol of liberalism.

BIBLIOGRAPHY

See above, the bibliographies for chaps. vi and ix. The volume by L.-P. Béranger (*Mémoires historiques et pièces authentiques sur M. de La Fayette* [Paris, 1790]) is by an admirer and was probably written with the collaboration of Lafayette himself, to enhance the general's popularity during the French Revolution. That by A.-H. de Lapierre de Châteauneuf (*Le Général Lafayette: mémoires authentiques* [Paris, 1831]) was likewise inspired by Lafayette; see below, p. 148, and n. 18. The story about Voltaire's kneeling to Adrienne, given on the testimony of these two authorities, may easily be questioned, since neither Lafayette's memoirs nor Adrienne's mention the episode, which could certainly not have been considered negligible by either of them. Moreover, Adrienne was not the type of person one would expect to find among the admirers of Voltaire. Yet because neither denied the anecdote, and especially because Lafayette, in approving both Béranger's and Châteauneuf's books, seemed to confirm it, it has been assumed here to be authentic.

[22] L. P. de Bérenger, *Mémoires historiques et pièces authentiques sur M. de la Fayette* (Paris, 1790), pp. 118–19; A. Châteauneuf, *Lafayette* (Paris, 1831), p. 49; but see the bibliographical note on this page.

[23] Gibbon to Holroyd, April 12, 1777, *The autobiography and correspondence of Edward Gibbon*, ed. Alex. Murray (London, 1869), p. 249.

[24] Vardill to Eden, May 29, 1777, Stevens, II, no. 164.

CHAPTER XII

Seeking a New World

W HEN the "Victoire" left the port of Los Pasajes, it
carried, besides a crew of about thirty men, Broglie's
officers, their servants, and several other passengers.[1]
The English agents in Paris reported to their government that
the boat was going to sail directly to Philadelphia,[2] despite the
fact that it had been registered at Bordeaux as bound for Santo
Domingo. It had indeed been the original intention of Lafayette and Dekalb to break their voyage at a Dominican harbor.[3] The rumor, however, that the king had sent out orders
to arrest the marquis at the ports of call in the West Indies determined them to risk the danger of an unbroken crossing to
the mainland. This was a counsel of desperation, for a trans-
atlantic crossing was a perilous venture at best. No one could
tell how long it might take. It had been known to last three
months and even longer. Water might give out, food might become contaminated, disease was no rare occurrence. A relatively large number of vessels never reached their destinations at
all. Only an inexperienced sailor would lightly consider going
uninterruptedly from Spain to the American continent.

Captain Le Boursier was, however, of a different opinion. He
had taken on all his passengers with the understanding that
they were going to Le Cap in Santo Domingo. When they had
registered with the port authorities at Bordeaux, testifying that
they were good Catholics—that is, not refugee Huguenots—and

[1] See Appen. VI.

[2] Bancroft to Wentworth, April 24, 1777, Stevens, I, no. 65; Stormont to Weymouth,
May 7, 1777, P.R.O., S.P., France 78/302, no. 82.

[3] Dekalb to Mme Dekalb, April 6, 1777, Colleville, p. 135.

that their purpose in leaving France was business or some other legitimate pursuit, they had all signified the intention of going to Santo Domingo. Le Boursier knew that this was the usual procedure of those who wished to avoid detection in their dealings with the American insurgents and that Santo Domingo was not their ultimate destination, but he had expected at least to call at Le Cap for supplies. Furthermore, he had brought on board, without consulting Lafayette, about eight thousand dollars' worth of goods, of which he hoped to dispose at Le Cap. He therefore demurred about carrying out Lafayette's orders to sail directly to the mainland. Lafayette, supported by his fellow-officers, threatened to take the command away from Le Boursier, if he did not obey. The captain reluctantly yielded, but when the marquis, discovering the real reason for Le Boursier's hesitation, also promised to make good any losses that he might incur on his cargo, the skipper's objections were entirely overcome and he steered the vessel straight for Charleston.

As the "Victoire" drew away from the Spanish shore the Marquis de Lafayette, with a sinking feeling, watched the land disappear upon the horizon. He thought of his wife and his little daughter and wondered how his family and friends had taken the news of his second departure. But reasoning that he would have been separated from them even if he had consented to go to Italy, he felt less apologetic. This step that he had taken, now irrevocable, was better than "dragging out a life without glory in the midst of the people most opposed both to his plans and to his manner of thinking."[4] Yet all the way across the ocean this conflict between regret and indignation went on within him.

Other things, however, soon began to occupy Lafayette's mind. He was a very bad sailor. His only previous experience upon the sea had been his Channel crossings and he had been frightfully sick on those. He was now very ill much of the first few weeks out. His only consolation was that many others on board fared just as badly as he. Contrary winds, alternating calms

[4] Lafayette to Mme Lafayette, May 30, 1777, *Mémoires*, I, 84–85.

and storms delayed the "Victoire." The inexperienced sailor
was terribly bored. For almost two months one day followed
another without variation of activity or scene. "Always the sky,
always the water and tomorrow the same routine. People who
write volumes on a sea-crossing must be awful drivellers."[5]

Nevertheless, there were occasional adventures to break the
monotony. The "Victoire" was heavy and inadequately armed.
She had only two bad cannon and a few muskets.[6] While a
man-of-war could be outrun, a privateer would be hard to elude.
Precautions were therefore necessary. What little defense could
be made, Lafayette prepared to offer, counting more on the
loyalty of his companions than the weapons at their disposal.
Suspecting that the English might be even more severe with him
than with any ordinary adventurer, he was prepared to blow
up the "Victoire" rather than surrender. He and his fellow-
passengers were therefore constantly on the *qui vive*.

They were very lucky at first. They saw some vessels, but
none of them gave chase. Their chief problem soon became the
less exciting one of finding some means to while away the time.
When his illness passed, Lafayette was content to amuse himself
by taking lessons in English and military tactics. He depended
upon Dekalb and Brice to teach him about the people and the
language he was to encounter; and almost any one of Broglie's
"caravan" (as Dekalb called the "Victoire" passengers)[7] knew
more about military tactics than he. After they had been several weeks at sea, he also tried to relieve the monotony by writing letters to his wife and father-in-law, though he knew that
they could not be received for several months yet to come.

Lafayette often wondered about Adrienne and his "children."
He wrote to her several times as the "Victoire" plowed her
course through the "sad expanse" of the Atlantic. He told her
how cruel he found the distance between them, how much the
ocean bored him, how right he felt his action to have been.

---

[5] *Ibid.*, pp. 86–87.

[6] *Mémoires*, I, 15, says "two cannon," though Castex says six; see Castex, "Pierre de
Basmarein," *Revue des questions historiques*, CII (1925), 95.

[7] Dekalb to Broglie, September 24, 1777, A.A.E., Corr. Pol., E.-U., II, 235 v.

The thought that she might not forgive him alone disturbed him. But she must remember, as he did, that Italy too was far away. Nor would he have been any safer there, for, except the chance of capture by the English while at sea, he really ran no risk. "The rank of general has always been regarded as a title to immortality." He would have been exposed to considerably greater danger in the French army. As a general in America he would be used only to give advice. So she must not worry. Turning to "more important things," he wondered whether their new baby was going to be a boy or a girl. She must not lose a minute in letting him know.

He alluded to Italy impatiently several times, but not once did he mention his earlier dread that he might be recaptured and made to return. Perhaps he had already forgotten about it, or perhaps it already seemed a little unbecoming in a major-general to have stolen away in disguise. As he tried to persuade Adrienne to see how much better was his decision to go to America than her father's proposal that he go to Italy, he used an argument that must have sounded strange to the aristocrats of the Noailles household. "You will admit, my heart, that the work and the life that I am embarking upon are quite different from those intended for me on that futile trip. Defending that liberty which I adore, freer myself than anyone, coming as a friend to offer my services to this very interesting republic, I bring to it only my sincerity and my good-will, without ambition or personal interest. In working for my glory, I work for their welfare. I hope for my sake you will become a good American. It is a sentiment meant for virtuous hearts. The welfare of America is intimately linked with the welfare of all humanity. She is going to become the respected and secure refuge of virtue, good character, tolerance, equality, and a peaceful liberty."[8]

Lafayette knew that his behavior must appear very foolish indeed to all those who were expected to read this letter. Here was a young man who had left a loving wife and family and had spent money recklessly in order to go off on an adventure that might take weeks and even months or perhaps end in a British

[8] Lafayette to Mme Lafayette, June 7, 1777, *Mémoires*, I, 88–89.

prison, only for the incredible purpose of bringing help to
rebels. How could the young marquis tell them—and especially
his wife—that he was tired of their patronage and their con-
descension? How could he explain that though he considered
himself a failure in everything he had so far attempted, he still
hoped for success somewhere? He had been content up to now
to use the argument of glory and the desire to learn the trade
of arms, though "the occasion to do something and to learn"
had failed to impress the Duc d'Ayen. Even his earlier letters
to Adrienne, whom he now urged to be a good republican, had
never mentioned a word about "the welfare of humanity" or
"equality and peaceful liberty." But these were stock phrases
that were in his atmosphere and that could be found, praised or
condemned, in almost every book that was published in his
country. Many young men of his day were learning to react to
them with unthinking hatred or devotion. They certainly were
familiar to Lafayette, and he could without conscious strain
take them up as if he had been used to them all his life.

Yet he had never before thought at such length and in
such unmistakable terms about his more idealistic motives for
going to America. If he knew anything of current literature—
if at this time he had even read any of Voltaire, Rousseau,
Raynal, upon whom he was later to talk so familiarly—he seldom hitherto had acted in accordance with their precepts. He
had lived the life of a typical court noble, concerned chiefly with
balls and receptions and military affairs, leaving to stewards
the care of his peasants and estates. The only time he had
expressed anything that seemed to be an opinion on politics,
except for his interest in America, was when, along with a group
of other young aristocrats, he had helped to make fun of Parlement at the moment when it was enjoying its greatest popular
support. The only "republican" action to his credit was his
refusal to take a position in the household of the Comte de
Provence; and the reason for that was described as "republican"
only about eight years later when he had already convinced
himself and was trying to prove to others how good a republican
he always had been. He forgot to tell the profound personal
motives that likewise entered into this decision.

But the Society of the Wooden Sword, where now he could remember "hardly ever having thought or heard anything which appeared to him worth saying,"[9] where only the awkwardness of his manner had distinguished him from other young aristocrats, seemed far away indeed from a frail bark tossed upon the waves of the Atlantic Ocean. Perhaps he and his companions had discussed such things as liberty and equality on board the "Victoire." A group of young men who had several dreary weeks before them on a slow-moving boat before they could put themselves at the disposal of a new rebellion might well have discussed the merits of the cause they were going to serve. Or perhaps Lafayette, between spells of sickness and lessons in English and strategy, had more fully developed his own philosophy. At any rate, though he had mentioned Italy several times in his first letter to his wife from shipboard (May 30), he had not then felt called upon to explain his preference for America in terms of "virtue," "good character," or "tolerance." On June 7, however, in his second epistle to Adrienne, he declared himself—somewhat prematurely—a full-fledged devotee of liberty. He had not yet stopped to think out clearly what liberty and equality might mean to him or to the world, nor was he for many years yet to come to be certain of the many implications of the liberal creed, but it helped to establish in his own mind a completely satisfactory rationalization of his conduct. Why had he gone to America instead of to Italy? Because he believed in the things for which America was said to be fighting? He did not really know that America was fighting for those things. He did know that she was fighting England, and that was enough to make him believe that he ought to be on her side.[10] He did not really know that liberty and equality were good. He did know that glory was good, at least for him, and since glory was to be found on the side of liberty and equality, they must be good too, especially since so many brilliant people were said to believe that they were. If by any chance England had been fighting to free the Negroes in the colonies and the colonies had revolted in opposition to this measure, Lafayette would not have mentioned "equality and a peaceful liberty" in

[9] *Ibid.*, p. 7.   [10] See Appen. IX below.

his letters to Adrienne, though he might still have been on the
"Victoire," sailing across the "sad expanse" of the Atlantic,
seeking high rank and glory by defiance of perfidious Albion.
But as England had solemnly been declared to be fighting
against the rights of man, Lafayette found himself decidedly in
favor of the rights of man. Thus, out of a few catchwords which
the American agents in Paris had exploited and the necessity for
finding a rational explanation of his own extravagant conduct
was born the liberalism of the foremost European exponent of
the liberal creed in the two succeeding generations. Hesitating
and apologetic as yet, it was to acquire the vigor and tenacity
of a conviction upon the new soil toward which the "Victoire"
was carrying him. He was somewhat surprised at it himself. He
wrote Adrienne, "I am becoming day by day extraordinarily
reasonable. You know that the vicomte keeps repeating that
travel molds young men; if he were to say it once every morning
and once every night, it would certainly not be too often, for I
feel more and more the justice of that remark."

By the time he closed this letter to Adrienne, there was a re-
vival of energy and interest on board the wind-tossed "Victoire." They had sighted some birds, and guessed that land
could not be far off. For several nights now, as they drew nearer
and nearer to the blockaded ports of the Carolinas, they had
sailed without lights. Forty leagues from the coast they were
badly scared. A small boat hove to, and they got ready to defend themselves against attack. She turned out to be an
American. They tried to keep up with her but she was too fast.
As they came closer to the shore, they spied at a distance two
other frigates which proved to be British cruisers blockading the
Charleston harbor. The food and water supply was now low, because they had been too liberal with it at first, and they had to
be very careful of it now. Nevertheless they wished to run no
unnecessary risks with either the English or the currents. Lafayette consequently preferred to find some less conspicuous
place than Charleston to land. They skirted the coast in a north-
erly direction for several days, looking for a chance to run the
British blockade. A strong northeasterly wind finally blew them

toward the shore and at the same time drove the English cruisers southward. They found a landing about twenty-five leagues from Charleston and determined to send a party ashore to secure a pilot. Lafayette, Dekalb, Brice, the mate of the "Victoire," and seven oarsmen went in the ship's launch to reconnoiter.

It was two o'clock in the afternoon when the small boat pulled away from the "Victoire." They met only some Negroes rowing a huge pirogue, and were able to discover that these were the slaves of a Major Huger of the South Carolina militia and that the port in which the "Victoire" had anchored was the Bay of Georgetown at the mouth of the Great Pedee River. They could learn very little about the country from the confused statements of the ignorant Negroes, but understood that the locality was unsafe because the English sometimes roved the neighboring estuaries and had only recently run off with some fishermen. They did not know how much credence to put in these rambling statements, but as the Negroes were willing to lead them to a pilot who they said lived at the head of the island, they allowed the slaves to precede in their pirogue while they rowed behind. Thus they traveled for hours up the bay until, at ten o'clock, the ebbing tide left their heavy launch stuck in the mud. They decided to leave their boat where it had stopped and to get into the Negroes' dug-out, directing the slaves to take them to the pilot and thence to their master.[11] Thus did Lafayette first set foot upon American soil. Local tradition still distinguishes the spot upon North Island where he landed.[12] It was Friday evening, the thirteenth of June, 1777. Eighty days had elapsed since the "Victoire" had left Bordeaux and fifty-four since she had put out from the Bay of Los Pasajes for the open sea.

Lafayette might very well have experienced a sense of religious awe and thanksgiving as he felt the ground of a new

[11] Dekalb to Mme Dekalb, June 15, 1777, Colleville, pp. 142–44; Kapp (pp. 109–10) somewhat inaccurately gives an account based upon this letter, which he misdates (p. 270) as of June 20, 1777.

[12] Henry A. M. Smith, "The barons of South Carolina," *South Carolina historical and genealogical magazine*, XIV (1913), 72.

hemisphere under his feet. Several years later, when he was himself firmly convinced that he had gone to America to fight for liberty and right, he declared that his first words on touching *terra firma* were an oath to conquer or to die with the American cause.[13] Nevertheless, within a few months, though that cause was far from won and he himself was thriving, he wrote Broglie and Duboismartin a letter which indicates that his newborn ardor for American ideals had not yet grown so vigorous as to crowd out all other emotions or so unabashed as to demand recognition from unsympathetic observers. Lafayette realized that the kind of language which would have stirred the devoted Adrienne to admiration would be only coldly received by his less idealistic friends. So he was content to explain to them how "grievously tormented" he was "by the desire to do something for his vanity and the advantage of his country," and how anxious to leave America in order to head an attack upon India or the British Antilles. News of a declaration of war upon England itself, he exclaimed, would decide him to leave for France immediately, even if he had to swim. There was no mention of the American cause here.[14] Like every good French military aristocrat, Lafayette was, when he wrote that letter, and even long afterward, chiefly concerned about beating the English. Despite a nascent liberal faith, he was interested in the American struggle primarily because to help America was the best way to harm the British and to win a reputation.

So if Lafayette breathed an oath to conquer or die in the American cause when first he trod on American soil, he merged the quarrel of America with that of France. He would conquer or die under the American banner, but not necessarily in America and certainly not alone because the American cause was a crusade for liberty and equality. In fact, when, the next October, he wrote Duboismartin about his plan to lead an attack upon the West Indies, he explained that he hoped "to fall

[13] *Mémoires*, I, 16.

[14] Lafayette to Duboismartin, October 23, 1777, Archives Nationales, AE[II] 1018; published also in *Musée des Archives Nationales* (Paris, 1872), pp. 617-18, no. 1018 (where it is wrongly stated that it is addressed to Broglie), and partially quoted in Doniol, II, 364; see also Appen. IX below.

upon some little English island whose Negroes would pay the cost of the enterprise." Though among American slaveholders themselves some of the more liberal had begun to object to the traffic in human beings, this remark was language which Duboismartin and Broglie would understand. That was the way in which a French noble of the sword was expected to think where England was concerned. It was language that Lafayette himself was in the course of time to come to regard as foreign to him, and, when that time came, he believed and wanted others to believe that at the moment he landed on American soil he was a devotee of liberal principles and the rights of man. But if he was, he had so far allowed only Adrienne and his American friends to know it.

It was to take time, attention, and harsh experience before the liberal gropings of a French aristocrat of the Old Régime could, on a freer soil and in a newer country, develop into an open conviction. He came to Carolina seeking glory and crying death to England. Those were old ideas that he had learned at Chavaniac among the portraits of his fallen ancestors. New ideas, however, had come glimmering as he learned to share the enthusiasm of American partisans in France and England, and grew more distinct as the "Victoire" left the European coast farther and farther behind and drew nearer and nearer to the scene of rebellion. They were to remain with him forever after, often neglected and not fully recognized at first, but soon to become so closely identified with him that his name became a symbol for future devotees of the new dispensation and himself the personification of their cause. Broglie had sent him forth to conquer an empire; he was to return a missionary of a new faith.

BIBLIOGRAPHY

For the events that took place on board the "Victoire," the letters of Lafayette, contained in his *Mémoires*, I, 84–97, are the chief source. Copies of these made by Mme Lafayette were exhibited at the Chicago Exposition of 1893; see *Catalogue de l'exposition historique des souvenirs franco-américains de la Guerre de l'Indépendance* (Paris, 1893), no. 32. The originals of the letters dated May 30–June 15, 1777, once were in the collection of Emmanuel Fabius (see p. 15 above); he informed me that there are no very essential differences between the copies made by Mme Lafayette and the text printed in the *Mémoires*. These letters must also be supplemented by the account of his venture given by Lafayette in 1783 or 1784 (*Mémoires*, I, 15–16) and during the Consulate (*ibid.*, p. 70). The narrative by Jared Sparks (*Writings of George Washington*, V, 449–50), which is the same as that in the second edition of Ducoudray-Holstein's *Lafayette* (pp. 33–34), is, as has already been explained, to be used with caution. In the Archives des Affaires Étrangères at Paris (Corr. Pol., E.-U., IV, 425–28 v.) is to be found a "copie d'un mémoire d'un des officiers françois passés en Amérique avec le Marquis de Lafayette, etc." (Dubuysson?) which gives some details about the voyage not otherwise available. It is also reproduced in Stevens' *Facsimiles*, VIII, no. 754. The account given in Kapp, *Johann Kalb*, pp. 109–10, and the letters written by Dekalb on June 15–18, 1777, upon which it is based (Colleville, pp. 141–51) are the best sources that we have on the landing of Lafayette. These should be supplemented by Lafayette's own descriptions, particularly that in his letters to Adrienne, June 19, 1777, *Mémoires*, I, 92.

The story given by Sparks about Lafayette's quarrel with his captain is corroborated by Lafayette's *Mémoires* (I, 70) and is therefore probably correct. On the other hand, the tale of pursuit by a ship sent from Bordeaux, which the younger Duboismartin gives in his memorial now in the Maryland Historical Society, is probably entirely fictitious, and that of mutiny on board the "Victoire," given in the (spurious) *Mémoires de Condorcet sur la Révolution française, extraits de sa correspondance et de celles de ses amis*, II (Paris, 1824), 49, confuses this voyage with Lafayette's return voyage on the "Alliance" in in 1779.

CHAPTER XIII

The Rise of a Legend

ABOUT a year after Lafayette first stepped into promi-
nence, John Adams, who had come to Paris to join
Franklin, attended a dinner at the home of the Duc
d'Ayen. There he found that the young Auvergnat, whose recent reputation for taciturnity and nonchalance had already
been forgotten, was now represented as "a youth of the finest
accomplishments and most amiable disposition." Adams was
assured "by some of the most intelligent men in France" that
the Marquis de Lafayette had been asked by a family council
of the Noailles to go to America! "The Marquis, ... hungry
for glory and desiring to distinguish himself in military service,
most joyfully consented and embarked in the enterprise. All
France pronounced it to be the first page in the history of a
great man."[1] The Noailles family council was, of course, a
myth, but that it should have been at all believed indicated
what a change had taken place within the year in the attitude
of that family toward the marquis. How amused Vergennes and
Maurepas must have been if they ever heard this version of the
marquis' adventure! It entirely justified the boy's intuitive
foresight just before the "Victoire" sailed out of the port of
Los Pasajes: "Once I am gone everybody will be of my opinion.
Once I have conquered, everybody will applaud my enterprise."[2]

Even the Duc d'Ayen, the last of his family to resist the
glamour of his son-in-law's renown, finally yielded. Shortly after

[1] C. F. Adams (ed.), *Works of John Adams*, III, 149 (entered under date of May 1,
1778).

[2] See above, p. 122.

the dinner with John Adams he wrote his charge a long-awaited letter filled with kindliness and friendly approval. To the young hero, who had now been in America over a year, it was a great victory indeed. "I love you too much," Lafayette impetuously replied, "not to be enchanted, overwhelmed with joy, whenever I receive from you any mark of kindness. You will find people who are more worthy of it, but I take the liberty of defying you to find anyone who appreciates or desires it more than I. . . . . I assure you that you will never again feel displeasure with me through any fault of mine."[3] That closed the incident as a family affair. But the dutiful son who thus made his peace with his family was by that time the cynosure of many eyes because of the very act for which he thus humbly apologized. A legend was in the making, and few helped to make it more than the subject of that legend himself.

Lafayette's extraordinary luck in reaching America despite the Duc d'Ayen, Maurepas, Louis XVI, and the British had made of him a sort of fatalist. He began to believe that destiny had marked him out for a great career. In the first leisurely letter that he had written to Adrienne from America he urged her to trust in his "star." "This star has just served me in a manner that astonishes everybody here. Count upon it, my heart, and rest assured that you ought to feel complete confidence in it."[4]

The sanguine young man's faith was to prove entirely justified. Despite many hardships and difficulties in the future, Lafayette was to be in many ways a favorite of the gods. Yet none of their favors was kinder than their granting him almost sixty years of life after he became a famous personage and a choice subject for eager biographers. This good luck enabled him to contribute in large part to what two generations of historians were to say about him. Their more important comments on his activities either were to be inspired or, if unfriendly enough, were to be more or less formally denounced by him. In future years public opinion was generally to respect him as a man of

[3] Lafayette to D'Ayen, September 11, 1778, *Mémoires*, I, 209–10.
[4] Lafayette to Mme Lafayette, June 19, 1777, *ibid.*, p. 92.

truth and integrity, even his enemies considering him too honorable or too naïve to lie consistently. Hence, for more than half a century after he first set foot on American soil, especially when in the 1820's and 1830's he was the only surviving major-general of the Continental Army, no other source of information regarding what had happened during that Revolution was considered more competent and reliable. As for his own part in those events, fortunate indeed was the historian who could have from the gallant volunteer's own mouth or pen the story of what had occurred.

Lafayette was highly accommodating in this regard. His earliest account of his first departure for America was written for some admiring friends only six or seven years after the event.[5] In subsequent narratives he added further details.[6] In these several versions of the story he made quite a romantic figure of himself. He had always had republican leanings, he said, and had burned to fight the Americans' fight ever since he first heard of the insurgent cause from the Duke of Gloucester's lips at the Comte de Broglie's dinner. Thereafter, no one could dissuade him. When it was explained to him how difficult it would be to secure transportation to the new world, he bought his own ship, the "Victoire." The government interfered, sent out a *lettre de cachet* for him, ordered the authorities at Bordeaux to stop him, and dispatched fast vessels to the French West Indies, with the command to arrest him if he got that far. He succeeded in sailing the "Victoire" to a nearby Spanish port, but there orders reached him from his king to return to France. He went back to Bordeaux, defied the ministers, and, in disguise, only after a very narrow escape at St. Jean-de-Luz regained his vessel and set sail.

To the young hero's admiring readers this story had every

[5] "Mémoires de ma main jusqu'en l'année 1780," *Mémoires*, I, 5–66, written in 1783 or 1784. Just previous to this he had modestly refused to speak for publication about his part in the American war; cf. Hilliard d'Auberteuil, *Essais historiques et politiques sur la Révolution de l'Amérique septentrionale*, II (Brussels, 1782), 425.

[6] "Sur le départ pour l'Amérique en 1777," *Mémoires*, I, 67–71; "Lettre à M. d'Hennings," *ibid.*, III, 219–69, of which the original manuscript is in the Huntington Library, HM 21654; it was also published separately as *Lettre du Général Lafayette au bailli de Ploen (15 Janvier 1799)*.

semblance of truth. Yet the letters Lafayette wrote just before
the "Victoire" put out to sea and as she crossed the ocean said
nothing about *lettres de cachet*, disguises, or pursuits. There was
good reason for silence on these matters. The *lettres de cachet*
had never materialized; the disguise and fear of pursuit seemed
somewhat grotesque on the part of a major-general in the light
of Mauroy's assurances and the ease with which he had made
good his escape. The first mention of vigorous official opposition
came only some years later, in the account written in 1783 or
1784. But from that time on, Lafayette insisted upon the
point. His statements in this regard were always true, yet created an erroneous impression, since he himself did not know the
extent to which some members of the government had connived
with his accomplices. In 1798, for example, he wrote to Washington that he had made his first trip to America "not only un-
licensed, but forbidden."[7] In 1799 when, as an exile in Germany, he wrote his autobiography, he again insisted that he had
acted against the wishes of his government.[8] In 1801 he informed the daughter of his companion, Dekalb, that while her
father's departure "was encouraged by the Comte de Broglie and
secretly approved by the French government," his own was accomplished at first "without the knowledge of the government
and soon after in spite of it."[9] When, moreover, John Marshall
in his *Life of Washington*[10] implied that the boy Lafayette had
come to America with the connivance of Louis XVI's government, the man Lafayette wrote a formal denial.[11] This denial,
however, was not published until after Lafayette's death, and
so in 1824–25 when he made a triumphal tour through the
United States, fêted and banqueted such as no one, not even
Washington, had ever been, collecting souvenirs and honorary
degrees, and keeping bookdealers and authors busy publishing

---

[7] Lafayette to Washington, August 20, 1798, Cornell University Library, Sparks
MSS; contained in garbled translation in *Mémoires*, IV, 435.

[8] "Lettre à M. d'Hennings, January 15, 1799," *loc. cit.*

[9] Lafayette to Mme Geymüller, May 1, 1801 (misdated by Kapp as of April 30,
1800), Kapp, p. 303.

[10] III (London, 1805), 410.   [11] *Mémoires*, I, 67–71.

volumes about him, several of the hastily compiled biographies assumed—as it seemed most logical to assume—that if the members of the French government had agreed to prevent his departure, he could not have made good his escape.[12] None of these tracts displeased him more than Ducoudray-Holstein's *Memoirs of General Lafayette*, which committed this offense.[13] Five thousand copies of the *Memoirs* were sold within a few months and its version of the Lafayette incident was spread throughout the country. Though, because of friendly regard for the author, Lafayette did not publicly deny his story, he saw Ducoudray-Holstein, set him right about what had happened,[14] and provided him with approved biographical materials;[15] and the second edition of Ducoudray-Holstein's *Memoirs* carried the censored version. The *Mémoires* of the Comte de Ségur, which appeared soon after (1825), lent corroboration to the revised story, although, for what had happened at Bordeaux in 1777, Ségur had had to depend on others' testimony.

The venerable revolutionary had already developed into almost a legendary figure when his American biographers came to ask him for the details of his career. Young George Ticknor[16] and Jared Sparks,[17] both destined to become eminent figures in the greatest university of the new world, learned from his own tongue how he had risked his government's displeasure and his father-in-law's ire to aid the failing cause of their infant country. Several youthful French liberals repeated the same inspired

[12] Cf., e.g., *American military biography; containing . . . . the life of Gilbert Motier La Fayette* ([Cincinnati], 1825), p. 274; *Memoirs of General La Fayette* (New York: Russell Robbins, 1825), p. 91.

[13] (New York, 1824), p. 16.

[14] Lafayette to Masclet, August 13, 1825, in the Gardner-Ball Collection, Indiana University Library.

[15] Ducoudray-Holstein, *Memoirs of Lafayette* (Geneva, 1835), preface.

[16] George Ticknor, *Outline of the principal events in the life of General Lafayette, from the "North American review"* (Boston, 1825) (translated into French [Paris, 1825] as *Histoire du Général de Lafayette par un citoyen américain*), pp. 5–8; the original article appeared as a review of the biographies by Ducoudray-Holstein and Regnault-Warin (see below, n. 18), *North American review*, XX (1825), 147–80. It had the distinct approval of Lafayette: see *Life, letters and journals of George Ticknor*, I (London, 1876), 285 and note.

[17] *Writings of George Washington*, V, 445–56.

story in their biographies of the revered leader.[18] And in England, refuting the disparagements of the *Quarterly review*, the sprightly Lady Morgan also presented the orthodox version.[19] Thus, during Lafayette's lifetime, the only accounts of what had taken place in 1777 to receive a respectful and unchallenged hearing were those directly influenced by Lafayette himself.

This was even more so after his death, since the old general, admired by his friends as a leader of liberal causes and respected by his enemies as a noble adversary, suffered at the hands of few skeptics and iconoclasts. Shortly after he died his family gathered the papers he had left behind, edited them with touching filiopietistic tenderness, and published them. The completed *Mémoires* contained several versions of the American venture—among others the account found in Sparks's then recently published *Writings of George Washington* (Boston, 1834). Sparks's narrative tallied almost word for word with that in the second edition of Ducoudray-Holstein, which appeared a few months later, and it is possible, unless Ducoudray-Holstein plagiarized Sparks, that both historians copied from a manuscript put at their disposal by their hero. Alone among Lafayette's friends, Comte Mathieu Dumas, who had been associated with him since the American war, let fall a hint that Lafayette, in embarking upon the "Victoire," had had, "if not the permission, at least the approbation of the king and his ministers."[20] Dumas' statement was itself a departure from strict veracity, but in the opposite direction, since it was not true that Louis XVI, or even all his ministers, had approved Lafayette's mission. In general, however, Dumas' memoirs were a eulogium of Lafayette, and this lone note of discord did not rise above the diapason of awe and admiration that a new generation

[18] Cf. M. Regnault-Warin, *Mémoires pour servir à la vie du Général La Fayette* (2 vols.; Brussels, 1824), I, 4–7; B. Sarrans jeune, *Lafayette et la Révolution de 1830* (2 vols.; Brussels, 1832), I, 1–4; A. Chateauneuf, *Lafayette* (Paris, 1831).

[19] Lady Morgan, *France in 1829–30* (London, 1830), pp. 61–101; cf. *Quarterly review*, XVII (1817), 278.

[20] *Memoirs of his own time*, I (Philadelphia, 1839), 14–15. Dumas added that he had himself intended to join Lafayette, but the French government had interfered at the last moment, because it was its interest "to dissemble the succor it afforded."

had come to feel for the hoary leader of the last. When Lafayette's daughter Virginie published her mother's memoirs
and her own reverent comments (1868), the legend received its
finishing touches.

Subsequently, almost unchallenged in Franco-American
circles, the belief that Lafayette had gone to America entirely of
his own accord and without any official collusion was accepted
by both historians and laymen.[21] The Germans, on the other
hand, respected no such legend. In 1839 Friedrich von Raumer
published his *Europa*, and revealed that Lord Stormont, the
English ambassador at Versailles, considered Vergennes, the
French foreign minister, definitely responsible for Lafayette's
behavior. And just before the Franco-Prussian War, a German
refugee in America named Friedrich Kapp, anxious to show
that America owed a huge debt of gratitude to Germany as well
as to France, wrote several books on the subject of German aid
to the American colonies, among which was a biography of
Dekalb. Kapp had discovered Dekalb's letters to his wife, and
out of them constructed a story which in many significant details differed from Lafayette's interpretation. Kapp's book
started a counter-legend. In his anxiety to prove that Lafayette
and Dekalb were equally accessory to the Comte de Broglie's
intrigue, the German biographer maintained that Lafayette had
been fully aware of Broglie's intentions from the moment of his
earliest association with Dekalb and had knowingly joined the
Broglie conspirators.

This version of the story never became commonly accepted,
for the French historians were to have the last inning. As the
hundredth anniversary of the French Revolution approached,
the French government decided to celebrate the century of revolution in both France and America, not only by an exchange of
statues of Liberty and a world-exposition, but also by publish-

---

[21] Cf., e.g., Ebenezer Mack, *Life of Gilbert Motier de Lafayette* (Ithaca, N.Y., 1841);
P. C. Headley, *The life of General Lafayette* (New York, 1856); Lydia Hoyt Farmer,
The life of La Fayette (New York, [1888]); Bayard Tuckerman, *Life of General Lafayette*
(2 vols.; New York, 1889); A. Bardoux, *La jeunesse de La Fayette, 1752–1792* (Paris,
1892). Bardoux, though acknowledging his indebtedness to Doniol (see below, p. 150),
actually depends chiefly upon Lafayette's *Mémoires*.

ing a thoroughly documented history of France's part in the establishment of American independence.[22] M. Henri Doniol, author of several studies of Lafayette and a friend of the surviving members of the great man's family, was charged with this work. He proceeded with admirable patience and zeal, and produced an impressive mass of significant material. He felt called upon, however, to re-establish Lafayette's prestige. Exploiting Kapp's findings, but basing his own interpretation largely upon the study of documents available in the archives of the French ministry of foreign affairs, Doniol came to a different conclusion. There had been close co-operation between Dekalb and Lafayette, he admitted, and possibly some of the French ministry were also privy to their plans. Still Dekalb was a conscious tool of Broglie, while Lafayette acted only out of the noblest motives and never suspected what either of them had in mind; Dekalb, besides, played a secondary rôle to Lafayette's "lead."

The cause of Franco-American solidarity was thus saved. Charlemagne Tower, formerly American ambassador at Paris, was engaged at about the same time in writing his *Lafayette in the American Revolution*,[23] and accepted without question Doniol's story of his hero's career up to the arrival in America. Étienne Charavay shortly afterward wrote his *Le Général La Fayette* and was likewise content to follow Doniol for this phase of his study. All of the several biographies that have appeared since Charavay have depended almost exclusively upon Lafayette, or Doniol, Tower, and Charavay regarding the 1777 venture.[24]

And so the single event in Lafayette's long career which is

[22] Doniol, I, i.

[23] (2 vols.; Philadelphia, 1895).

[24] Cf. George Morgan, *The true La Fayette* (Philadelphia, 1919); Joseph Delteil, *Lafayette* (New York, 1928), pp. 3–56; Jacques Kayser, *La vie de La Fayette* (Paris, 1928), pp. 9–30; Henry Dwight Sedgwick, *La Fayette* (Indianapolis, 1928), pp. 1–31; John Simpson Penman, *Lafayette and three revolutions* (Boston, 1929), pp. 1–27; Brand Whitlock, *La Fayette* (2 vols.; New York, 1929), I, 3–69; Michael de La Bedoyere, *Lafayette: a revolutionary gentleman* (London, 1933), pp. 13–35. Of these, however, Whitlock has used additional information gleaned from the letters of Dekalb, given more fully than by Kapp, in Colleville, *Missions secrètes*; and La Bedoyere has been somewhat critical of the Lafayette legend.

most familiar to the American schoolboy continued to be known almost as Lafayette had wished it to be. The youth who, out of republican convictions, risked life, fortune, and liberty to lead a loyal handful of men across perilous seas to fight on the side of virtue and right despite the combined efforts of his own government and England, has become the symbol of the good-will existing between the French and American republics. Yet his motives were not entirely "republican"; he followed rather than led, though he provided the means to go; virtue and right entered his mind only as an afterthought; and he might have guessed, if he had not preferred to remain deluded, that the risk he ran from his own government was not so great as their public behavior seemed to indicate. For in Lafayette's own time the good-will of the French government was almost entirely on the American side (or rather its ill-will entirely on the English side). The ministry accordingly did as little as it dared to interfere with his departure, and some of them discreetly blinked, or went so far as to promote, his activity. Even Doniol's Gallophile scrutiny of the papers in the French archives suggested this possibility to him, but left him unconvinced. Careful exploitation of Lord Stormont's and other English agents' dispatches would have confirmed this suggestion. Knowledge of the memoirs and correspondence of Montbarey, La Marck, Lameth, Lieutenant Duboismartin, and Carmichael would have assured him of its validity. And a more critical analysis of the letters of Dekalb, Deane, the older Duboismartin, and Lafayette himself would have made assurance doubly sure.

The principal source for the thesis of vigorous, republican leadership against active governmental opposition is Lafayette's own testimony. Yet Lafayette, as time went on, unconsciously tended to wrap his youthful years in a glamour and a light that never was, on sea or land. He quite naturally remembered only those anecdotes about his childhood that showed an independent and liberal character. He forgot to indicate how he had failed to establish himself satisfactorily in the position that his wealth and his wife's family's influence entitled him to expect. He minimized his associations with Dekalb and the Comte de

Broglie. He exaggerated the king's order to return into a *lettre de cachet*. And he neglected to mention Mauroy's assurance that the ministers would not seriously interfere with his departure. The editors of his several memoirs, moreover, often tampered with his own text, and he was besides not always adequately, even when correctly, informed.

Only one conclusion therefore seems possible. Although there is not a single word of deliberate untruth in any of Lafayette's versions of his adventure, the roseate impression that he gave the world of his exploits was certainly neither the whole truth nor wholly true. Yet Lafayette himself very sincerely believed every iota of it. And his obvious sincerity has been the foundation of a great saga. It is a beneficent saga, to be sure, but largely legendary none the less.

BIBLIOGRAPHY

The entry here given as from John Adams' *Diary* is actually inserted by his grandson, who edited his works, from a composition of a later date. It is highly probable, therefore, that Adams learned his story of the Noailles family council which sent Lafayette off to America from later and less significant conversations rather than at the dinner of May 1, 1778. Nevertheless, as an indication of the rising legend, it loses no value even so.

Doniol (II, 393) maintains that Lafayette himself argued that he was encouraged by his own government to go to America. This is derived from Doniol's misunderstanding of Marshall's statement that Lafayette left France "ostensibly in opposition to his sovereign" (*Life of Washington*, III, 410). Leaving out the word "ostensibly" from his translation of this phrase, Doniol finds that Lafayette must have believed that the government of France actually supported him, because he argued against the statement that he left "in opposition to his sovereign." This is, however, exactly the opposite to what Lafayette did say (*Mémoires*, I, 67).

For a more complete bibliography of works on Lafayette see Stuart W. Jackson, *La Fayette: a bibliography* (New York, 1930), and Louis Gottschalk, "Lafayette," *Journal of modern history*, II (1930), 281–87. The preceding chapter is a fuller development of my "Did the French government aid Lafayette's American adventure of 1777?" in the *Résumés des communications présentées au Congrès International des Sciences Historiques* (Warsaw, 1933), I, 161–64.

APPENDIX I

Lafayette, LaFayette, or La Fayette?

The biographers of Lafayette have spelled his name in any of these three fashions. Some have also used *De la Fayette*. The confusion is due to the fact that contemporaries, many of them people who knew Lafayette personally, did not know how to spell his name. Orthography of proper names was not as strict in the eighteenth century as it is now. The exact spelling of more than one of them is still a matter of dispute. Many of Lafayette's contemporaries were led to spell his name *La Fayette* because that was how his famous ancestor Mme de La Fayette, the novelist, had written it, and because the land from which the title was derived was called *La Fayette*.[1]

Lafayette's own immediate ancestors, however, always wrote *Lafayette*. A letter once in the possession of M. Emmanuel Fabius (see p. 15 above), dated Paris, February 15, 1726, is addressed to *La Marquise de Lafayette à Brioude* and signed *Lafayette*. It was probably written by Lafayette's grandfather Edouard. The Gardner-Ball Collection (Indiana University Library) contains a letter dated Brioude, October 26, 1743 or 1753, which is also signed *Lafayette*. This can be no other than Lafayette's father. In short, whatever evidence we have regarding the spelling of the name by Lafayette's immediate ancestors indicates that it was *Lafayette*.

The great abundance of autograph materials left by Lafayette himself makes the problem somewhat more, rather than less, complicated. The difficulty in his particular case arises from the fact that there is no way of telling whether his *f* is an *F* or an *f*. He always made it in the same way, whether he was writing *France* or *fils*, or similar words. Consequently, it is impossible to say whether he meant his name to be *LaFayette* or *Lafayette*. The possibility of the former is increased by the fact that he frequently used the abbreviation *L. f.* or *L. F.* Since in this abbreviation there is almost always a period between the *L* and the *F*, the chance of its being an *F* rather than an *f* is augmented (though Mme Lafayette and he sometimes used the abbreviation without a period).[2] It should also be noted that Lafayette owned a signet ring upon which there was the monogram *L F*,[3] and that he sometimes sealed his

[1] See Gerard to Mlle du Motier, December 28, 1774, University of Chicago Library, DC 146, f. L2 A3, Vol. I; receipt of Mme de La Fayette, January 28, 1686, Pierpont Morgan Library, New York City, "Outline French Revolution," III, 128; for an interesting controversy on the spelling of the marquis' name, see the "Mailbag" in the Paris *New York Herald*, May 17–21, 1934.

[2] Cf., e.g., Mme Lafayette to Bollman, May 22, 1796, in Huntington Library, HM 9417; Lafayette to "My dear friend," copy but indorsed in corner "true copy Lf.," in University of Chicago Library, DC 146, f. L2 A3, Vol. VII.

[3] Cloquet, p. 184.

letters with it.[4] From these facts it would seem that the general spelled his name *LaFayette*.

The chief reason for not accepting this spelling is that none of his family ever spelled it that way. In the printed documents which passed under the eye of Lafayette himself, the name is almost always spelled *Lafayette*, never *LaFayette*. The former is the spelling invariably used in the *Mémoires*, whose publication was supervised by his family, and in *Le Général Lafayette à ses collègues de la Chambre des Députés* (Paris, 1832), which he himself supervised. Mme de Lasteyrie uses it also in her book. The confusion can only be explained by assuming that Lafayette himself was indifferent as to whether the name was read *LaFayette* or *Lafayette*. Sometimes he considered the *F* a capital letter and sometimes a small letter, though apparently almost never the former in print. The name therefore may be either *LaFayette* or *Lafayette*, but *La Fayette* is impossible, as the general never left a space between the *La* and the *Fayette*. The spelling *Lafayette* has been followed consistently throughout this book as being the one which the general apparently preferred for printed publications.

The explanation sometimes given that Lafayette spelled his name *La Fayette* before the abolition of titles during the French Revolution and *Lafayette* afterward is based upon two inadequate arguments. In the first place, Ducoudray-Holstein says so (2d ed., p. 13 n.), but his testimony, here as always, is suspect. In the second place, Mme Lafayette before the Revolution used to sign *Noailles de la Fayette*[5] and *Noailles Lafayette* afterward.[6] This, however, no more proves that Lafayette signed *La Fayette* before the Revolution than that he signed *la Fayette*, though no one asserts the latter. There is no letter extant in which the signature is *La Fayette*. It is sometimes written before the Revolution as *Du Motier de Lafayette*,[7] sometimes *Marquis de Lafayette*, and most often *Lafayette* (or, in all these cases with a capital *F*, not preceded by a space). After the French Revolution one finds *Lafayette* (or *LaFayette*) most often and sometimes *L.f.* (or *L.F.*), but whether before or after the Revolution it is never *La Fayette*. Nevertheless, this last spelling has the sanction of good usage by some very fine historians, who, however, either gave the matter little thought or were influenced by the usual practice of the older branch of the family.

[4] See, e.g., Lafayette to Maubourg, [1789], Archives Nationales, F⁷ 4767.

[5] Cf. Mme Lafayette to [Pulaski], May 27, [1777], in Jackson Collection; and to Mangin, [1789], Mosnier, *Château Lafayette*, facsimiles in back of book.

[6] E.g., letter of May 22, 1796, *loc. cit.*

[7] Once, indeed, is to be found *Gilbert du Motier Mⁱˢ de Lafayette*; see Doniol, "Correspondance inédite de Lafayette avec le Comte d'Estaing," *Revue d'histoire diplomatique*, VI (1892), 406.

APPENDIX II

Lafayette and the Comtesse de Hunolstein

That Lafayette was in love with some fair lady in the winter of 1776 cannot be doubted. Ségur[1] is our authority for this statement. Since Ségur's *Mémoires* were published in 1825, while Lafayette was still alive, and since Lafayette, who did not hesitate to refute other writers' statements, never objected to Ségur's, Lafayette's silence on this score suggests acquiescence in Ségur's account.

The only problem is to identify the lady in question. It was not until seven years after 1776 that Lafayette's name was publicly associated with Mme de Hunolstein's. In 1774 that lady had been generally believed *d'une réputation intacte*,[2] but by 1783 her conduct was such an open scandal that even her mother considered her unworthy to continue in the service of the Duchesse de Chartres.[3] At that date it was a subject of common gossip at the Opéra that Lafayette was her accepted lover and that he had been enamored of her even before he went to America. Such gossip might be entirely disregarded as vicious or mistaken. In fact, Doniol[4] insists that Lafayette is confused in this regard with a certain Chevalier Armand de la Rouerie, and claims that this confusion is due to libelers after 1789. Yet Bachaumont wrote before 1789, and among those who told the same story after 1789 was also the Comte d'Espinchal, whose notes lie, still unpublished for the most part, in the Library of Clermont-Ferrand. Espinchal may have learned this story only from the Bachaumont account of it. On the other hand, it must be remembered that he was an Auvergne noble himself, knew Lafayette, and was considered one of the best-informed men of his day.[5] The probability of Espinchal's account being independent of Bachaumont's is enhanced by the circumstance that Bachaumont, who was merely repeating gossip, misspells the lady's name and calls her the Comtesse du Nolstein, whereas Espinchal gives it correctly.

Another almost contemporary reference to the episode is that of Marat.[6] Marat in 1791 accused Lafayette of trying to destroy the Duc d'Orleans (the former Duc de Chartres), because of the unforgiven humiliation Lafayette had suffered to the duke's advantage at the hands of the "Comtesse de

[1] I, 106.

[2] [Métra], *Correspondance secrète, politique et littéraire, etc.*, I, 20.

[3] Bachaumont, XXIII (1784), 32–33 (under date of June 30, 1783).

[4] "Enfance de Lafayette," *loc. cit.*, p. 28.

[5] "Madame du Barry: souvenirs du Comte d'Espinchal," *Review retrospective*, VI (1887), 193 n.; "Lafayette jugé par le Comte d'Espinchal," *ibid.*, XX (1894), 289–91.

[6] *Ami du peuple*, no. 440 (April 26, 1791), pp. 4–5.

Nolstein." But Marat borrowed his story of this episode from Bachaumont.[7] From the independent sources available, it nevertheless seems established that Lafayette was one of the Duc de Chartres' circle;[8] that he was in love with a *dame aimable autant que belle* in 1776;[9] that Mme de Hunolstein, who likewise belonged to that circle, was described in similar terms (*une des plus jolies et des plus agréables personnes de Paris*) by Espinchal;[10] that Bachaumont and Espinchal state that he was in love with Mme de Hunolstein (though it is barely possible that both are derived from the same source or from each other); and that their story or stories fit in very well with the account that Ségur gave and which Lafayette never denied.

The spurious "Condorcet" too says that it was for a lady's sake that Lafayette went to America, though he thinks she was Mme de Simiane.[11] Lida Rose McCabe,[12] following Condorcet, also mistakenly puts the Mme de Simiane episode at this time; and La Bedoyere[13] implies the same. But there is no evidence of any relations between Lafayette and Mme de Simiane before his departure for America.[14]

[7] *Ibid.*, p. 5 n.   [9] Ségur, I, 106.

[8] Bacourt, I, 63.   [10] "Lafayette," *loc. cit.*

[11] See [Marquis de La Rochefoucauld], *Mémoires de Condorcet sur la Révolution, extraits de sa correspondance et de celles de ses amis*, II, 57.

[12] *Ardent Adrienne: the life of Madame de La Fayette* (New York, 1930), pp. 62–63.

[13] *Lafayette*, p. 22.

[14] Since the first printing of this book, I have given a fuller account of the Comtesse de Hunolstein in *Lady-in-waiting: the romance of Lafayette and Aglaé de Hunolstein* (Baltimore, 1939).

APPENDIX III

Why Was Lafayette "Réformé" in 1776?

Until Charavay (p. 7) called attention to it, it had escaped the notice of all Lafayette's biographers that Lafayette had been placed in reserve in 1776. Charavay believed this was due to a voluntary act on Lafayette's part, undertaken in order to make it possible for him to go to America without incurring the charge of desertion. All the writers on Lafayette since Charavay, if they have not ignored the episode entirely, have accepted his explanation.

It nevertheless does not stand up under closer examination. The rush on the part of French officers to enter the service of America did not begin until Silas Deane arrived in Paris. That was on June 25, 1776, and Lafayette was *réformé* on June 11. Moreover, Lafayette, if he had still been in the service, might, like the Vicomte de Noailles and Dekalb, have asked for permission to go. Only if the ministers then refused to grant him leave would there have been any necessity to have himself put on reserve. Furthermore, being on reserve did not relieve him of the charge of desertion. A "reformed" officer was naturally no freer to accept service in a foreign army than a regular was.

The best argument, however, against believing Lafayette's partial withdrawal from the army a voluntary act is that it never raised any comment. For a son-in-law of the Noailles to withdraw from the Noailles Dragoons was certainly no trivial matter. The ministers, his subordinates, and someone in Lafayette's regiment would certainly have learned about it. The Duc d'Ayen, the Prince de Poix, and the Vicomte de Noailles were all his fellow-officers. How could they have failed. to notice the absence of their relative from the maneuvers of 1776? And since his father-in-law opposed Lafayette's going to America, he certainly would have wanted to know the reason for this absence. Some correspondence, some explanation, would have been forthcoming, and would have been recorded in some fashion in the war department. But it never was mentioned, whether in Lafayette's *états de service*, or by Lafayette himself, or by any of his contemporaries. It must have been, therefore, quite a routine affair, not so unusual as to excite comment. We know from several sources that for captains to be *réformés* by the Comte de St. Germain was quite a regular occurrence in 1776.[1]

There is also some direct evidence to indicate that Lafayette was at this time discontented with his career in the French army. The general dissatisfaction of young officers with St. Germain's policies was currently given as one reason for the alacrity with which so many of them offered their services to

[1] See Simonde de Sismondi, *Histoire des Français* (Brussels, 1844), XX, 241, and note; *Mémoires de M. le Comte de St.-Germain* (Amsterdam, 1779), 66–69, 120–24, 136, 178–79, 213–14, 235–38.

the United States.² The Marshal de Noailles had been one of the military authorities who protested most vigorously against the war minister's reforms.³ In fact, when Lafayette took flight from Bordeaux, there was, according to one contemporary, so loud an outcry against St. Germain that the young marquis' relatives took advantage of the opportunity once more to point out to the king "the harm that M. de St.-Germain had done to his service."⁴ All this tends to support the thesis that Lafayette had been forced out of the regular army by some act of the Comte de St. Germain.

Another possible explanation of the "reformation" of Lafayette is that it was done in expectation of his joining the Comte de Provence's staff. This would, partially at least, explain the silence of the records and other contemporary sources, since his leave would in that case have been granted with the consent of the Noailles. The arguments against this thesis are two. First, there was no real reason why a young officer on active duty could not also be on the staff of a prince. Second, the masque ball at which Lafayette and Provence quarreled, even if it occurred as late as 1776, probably came in the festive season before Lent when most of the gala occasions in Paris took place and therefore preceded the "reformation" by at least several months. But it may even have taken place before 1776. The only contemporary, besides Lafayette and Cloquet (see above p. 48), to mention the quarrel of Lafayette and Provence—John Quincy Adams,⁵ who perhaps learned of the episode from Lafayette—implies that Lafayette, asked to choose between a position in the prince's household and a commission in the army, selected the army. Since none of Lafayette's commissions during this period came after 1775, the quarrel probably took place in 1775 as narrated above (pp. 47–48). This probable date is supported by Lafayette's own statement⁶ that the episode took place before he learned of the American struggle. That, as we have seen (p. 50), was in the summer of 1775. In any case, the interval between the possible offer by Provence and the *réforme* was probably too long to permit the first to be considered the cause of the second. It was St. Germain rather than Provence who must be held responsible.

² Ségur, I, 101; *Journal de Métra*, IV, 267 (under date of April 2, 1777), which is the same as *Correspondance secrète inédite sur Louis XVI, etc.*, I, 40 (under date of April 3).

³ Alph. Jobez, *La France sous Louis XVI*, I (Paris, 1877), 460.

⁴ *Correspondance secrète inédite sur Louis XVI, etc.*, I, 43 (under date of April 10).

⁵ Adams, *Oration on the life and character of Gilbert Motier de Lafayette*, p. 15.

⁶ *Mémoires*, I, 8.

APPENDIX IV

Did Madame Lafayette Know of Lafayette's Proposed Departure?

Jared Sparks[1] says that Lafayette's wife "approved of his enterprise from the beginning, and threw no obstacles in his way." This is the only essential regard in which Ducoudray-Holstein's second edition departs from Sparks's text in narrating the story of Lafayette's escape, and then only to tell a more detailed, not a different, story. On pages 31–32 Ducoudray-Holstein says that Lafayette communicated to Adrienne his intention to sail for America before he actually left. "Thunderstruck with astonishment and apprehension, she was strongly opposed to her husband's departure; but seeing Lafayette's fixed determination to lose not a moment, she at once announced to him her desire to accompany him, and share with him all the perils of the sea and of the camp. It was now *his* turn to dissuade *her* from her resolution; and thus these two truly enthusiastic and heroic souls contended, during an hour's time, who should surpass the other in noble and generous feelings. At last Madame de Lafayette gained the palm; she wiped off her tears, promised not only to remain with her father, but assisted him [Lafayette] secretly, with a truly heroic zeal, to prepare everything for his voyage. She therefore did not join in these outcries against him: she wrote him a letter full of approval, love and encouragement. He said to me, it was an angelic letter, and confessed that if she had given him the least hint to return to her—'je n'aurais su trop que faire. J'étais ému, presque repentant.'" The author seems to be speaking upon the authority of Lafayette, with whom he was on fairly friendly terms.[2] When considered in the light of Dekalb's statement that he saw Lafayette in November, 1776, at the Noailles hôtel in Mme de Lafayette's presence,[3] this account would seem to be altogether authentic. But by the time Dekalb made this statement, Lafayette had already admitted to him that he had kept the entire matter secret from his wife.[4] Dekalb's testimony must therefore be considered as on the whole in favor of the thesis that Adrienne knew nothing of her Gilbert's intentions.

Mme de Lafayette herself insisted that she never knew about the contemplated departure until after it had taken place. At the top of the copy of Lafayette's letters which she probably made before 1785 for Dr. Breuil,[5] she

---

[1] *Writings of George Washington*, V, 448.   [2] See above, p. 147.

[3] Dekalb to St. Paul, November 7, 1777, *loc. cit.*

[4] Dekalb to Mme Dekalb, April 6, 1777, Kapp, p. 106.

[5] See *Mémoires*, I, vii, and n. 2; this copy was in the possession of Emmanuel Fabius, of Paris (see p. 15 above).

wrote that she did not know of Lafayette's plans, and the letters of Lafayette before he sailed seem to indicate that he expected her to be surprised by his procedure.[6] Moreover, in her memoirs of the Duchesse d'Ayen,[7] she also says that his departure was a cruel surprise to her. Besides, when one recalls that Mme de Lafayette was in an advanced stage of pregnancy at the time Lafayette left, the probability of her gently contesting with her husband for the privilege of going with him on a long sea voyage is greatly diminished. The explanation may then be that Holstein either confused some details which Lafayette gave him or romanticized; or perhaps Lafayette romanticized when talking to Holstein in 1824.

Another possible explanation is that up to December, 1776—that is, until the Vicomte de Noailles was officially refused permission to go to America— the Duc d'Ayen thought of embarking together with his two sons-in-law.[8] Both Lafayette and Noailles gave Dekalb the impression that they had D'Ayen's consent. In keeping with this interpretation, Adrienne would have been told about the plan, and this would explain how Dekalb could safely interview her husband even in her presence. After Noailles found he could not go, the family, in accordance with this possible explanation, felt that Lafayette ought not to go either, and went upon the assumption that he would not. For that reason, not knowing that he had continued his preparations for the venture even after December, 1776, they were surprised at his final departure, Adrienne no less than the others. This latter interpretation would explain the apparent contradiction in Holstein's and Mme de Lafayette's testimony, but would not take sufficiently into account the consistent hostility of the Duc d'Ayen to Lafayette's departure. It therefore seems more probable that Holstein wove his story out of whole cloth, that Adrienne paid no attention to, or did not understand, what Dekalb and her husband discussed when she was present, and that she really knew nothing about Lafayette's plans from start to finish.

[6] See above, pp. 94–95, 121–22.   [7] Lasteyrie, p. 57.

[8] Dekalb to Mme Dekalb, April 6, 1777, Kapp, p. 106.

APPENDIX V

Dates of Lafayette's Contracts with Deane

It has generally been believed by Lafayette's biographers that Noailles, Ségur, and he had a personal interview with Deane in August, 1776. This belief is based upon Deane's statement to the Committee of Secret Correspondence that he "told" several young men, whose names he does not mention, but whom he describes as "nearly connected with the court," that only their merit was important to Congress.[1] It may be that Deane had Lafayette and his two friends in mind, since Ségur says that they were the first nobles of the court to offer their services to America.[2] There is no proof, however, that Deane spoke to them personally. Ségur does not necessarily imply this in his noncommittal phrase, "our arrangements with the American commissioners." The fact that none of the three spoke English and Deane's French was bad also makes it improbable. On the other hand, Dekalb in his letter to St. Paul[3] says that it was he who introduced Lafayette to Deane, and only several months later. This statement is confirmed by Lafayette.[4] Lafayette, in fact, implies that he had earlier been *indirectly* in touch with Deane, for he says, "Wishing to address myself *directly* [italics mine] to Deane, I made the acquaintance of Kalb .... who acted as my interpreter."

If any arrangement was reached in August, 1776, it seems perfectly clear that it was vague and indirectly attained. No definite agreement was made until Lafayette alone signed the first of his two contracts with Deane. Dekalb says this was at the end of November.[5] But as this contract still exists, clearly dated, without erasure or correction, December 7, 1776,[6] this appears to be a *lapsus memoriae* on Dekalb's part. The first written contract of Lafayette was undoubtedly signed on December 7, 1776.

The second written contract of Lafayette with Deane was the list of thirteen agreed upon to sail on the "Victoire." It has long been known that the date December 7, 1776, placed on this document did not indicate the actual time of its composition.[7] The reason for this doubt was that the list quite obviously was drawn up after Lafayette was definitely in a position to

[1] August 15 [or 18?], 1776, Wharton, II, 124.   [2] Ségur, I, 104.

[3] November 7, 1777, *American historical review*, XV (1910), 563–64.

[4] *Mémoires*, I, 11.

[5] Dekalb to St. Paul, November 7, 1777, *loc. cit.*, p. 564.

[6] See above, pp. 74–76.

[7] Cf. Doniol, II, 379–80, and Tower, I, 35–36 n., who believe the contract was signed in February, 1777.

head an expedition, and this could not have been before he had bought the "Victoire." Lafayette, however, did not discover that his boat had been purchased until February 11, 1777, and he left for England on February 16 (see above, pp. 87–89). The details of the sale were not yet completed by that time (see above p. 93). Moreover, Lafayette, who was taking extraordinary pains not to be seen in the company of the Americans, would certainly have avoided a meeting in Paris with both Dekalb and Deane. It is therefore unlikely, though possible, that the final contract with Deane was made before the marquis' departure for London, as is generally stated. It is much more probable that only upon his return to France, or, in other words, while he was at Chaillot (March 13–16), did Lafayette, Dekalb, and Deane, represented by Carmichael, complete the details of their arrangement, antedating the final document as of Paris, December 7, 1776. This theory is confirmed by the reference of Lafayette, when in Maryland in 1824, to Carmichael as the man "who first received the secret vows of my engagement in the American cause,"[8] since, if these "vows" had been taken in Paris, Deane rather than Carmichael would have "received" them.

[8] Newspaper clipping from unknown source, giving Lafayette's reply to the Committee from Queen Ann's County, in L.C., House of Rep. papers, no .93.

APPENDIX VI

The Passengers on the "Victoire"

On account of the laws prohibiting Huguenots from leaving France, prospective passengers on vessels clearing French harbors were expected to register with the local port authorities. The record of the "Victoire's" passengers has been preserved and now is to be found in the Archives départementales de la Gironde at Bordeaux. A transcription has been given by Doniol (II, 384–85, 419–20); photostats of it are available at the Library of Congress, Division of Manuscripts; and translations have been furnished by Miss Elizabeth S. Kite.[1] From this record it appears that the following persons declared their intention of sailing on the "Victoire":

MARCH 21, 1777: Dekalb, Duboismartin, De la Colombe, Bedaulx, Candon, Franval, Gimat, Brice
MARCH 22, 1777: De Vrigny, Rousseau de Fayols, Delesser, Valfort, Gilbert du Motier (Lafayette), Camus and Moteau (his servants), Argé (or Rogé) (Dekalb's servant), Redon
MARCH 24, 1777: Capitaine, Dubuysson, Lepas

Each of these, more or less accurately, answered questions as to full name, place of origin, height (i.e., short, medium, or tall), color of hair, age, and destination. All declared (excepting Dubuysson and Capitaine—and they probably omitted to do so only by oversight) that they either "professed the Catholic religion" or were "Catholics of long standing" (*anciens Catholiques*). All declared that they were going to Santo Domingo or, more specifically, to Le Cap (i.e., Cap-Haytien), and some of them stated that their reason for going was "business."

That this registration was a mere formality is shown by the carelessness with which it was performed. The inaccurate description of Lafayette has already been given.[2] In addition to the failure to record the religion of Dubuysson and Capitaine at all, there is the fact that Dekalb, who was a Protestant,[3] was described as professing the Catholic religion. Edmund Brice was an American and probably also a Protestant, but, for motives that are not clear, described himself as Leonard Price, born at Sauveterre, in France. It may perhaps be that he was born in Europe, though of American parentage, as has been suggested.[4] But it seems more likely that for some reason or other he felt it wise to practice deception. Bedaulx, who registered as a native of Neuf-

---

[1] "Lafayette and his companions," *loc. cit.*, pp. 25–27.

[2] See above, p. 100.

[3] Kapp, p. 36.   [4] Kite, *loc. cit.*, p. 21.

châtel in Switzerland, is nevertheless described by Lafayette as a Dutchman.[5]

More confusing than these minor irregularities is the failure of some of the passengers to affix their signatures to the record. Sometimes when a passenger on another vessel was unable to write, this fact was indicated as the reason for his not signing the register. In the case of the passengers on the "Victoire," however, five of them (Gimat, Moteau, Argé or Rogé, Redon, and Lepas) did not sign, and no reason was given. Only one servant (Camus) signed. Gimat was the only officer who failed to do so. Moteau was another of Lafayette's servants, and Argé was Dekalb's. There is no indication of who Redon and Lepas were. Dekalb, however, enumerated to his wife (April 6) six boat officers, a surgeon, and a cook; and since the boat officers apparently did not register, it is possible that Redon and Lepas were the surgeon and the cook in question.

Not counting Lepas, Redon, and the servants, all the men who registered at Bordeaux were on the list which Deane and Lafayette had drawn up before the latter's departure,[6] with the exception of Dubuysson. Dubuysson was one of Broglie's men and had been included on the roll of officers who were to have sailed from Le Havre in December, 1776. In addition, Dekalb, Fayols, Duboismartin, De Vrigny, and Candon were on the original list prepared by Dekalb. When Mauroy joined the party in Spain, seven out of the fifteen officers on board the "Victoire" had figured on that list. Moreover, as Dekalb wrote his wife from Los Pasajes, Capitaine had also been "recommended to the marquis by the Comte de Broglie";[7] and Bedaulx had been suggested the previous December to Deane by Dekalb.[8] They were all under Dekalb's orders, the baron himself said; he afterward called them Broglie's "caravan," and felt answerable to Broglie for their welfare.[9] Apparently more than half of the officers on the "Victoire" when finally she sailed from Los Pasajes frankly considered themselves Broglie's appointees. The others were Lafayette, Delesser, Valfort, Franval, Gimat, La Colombe, and Brice. Even of these Franval was, either now or later, in the confidence of Broglie's secretary, Duboismartin.[10] Delesser at least had official inducement to go, for he had received the brevet of colonel upon volunteering for service in America.[11]

[5] *Mémoires*, I, 15; cf., however, Kite, *loc. cit.*, p. 21. In petitions to Congress, dated February 2 and 4, 1778, Bedaulx speaks of Holland as if it were his home; Library of Congress, papers of the Continental Congress, no. 78, II, fols. 375–79. (I am indebted to Miss Kite for knowledge of these petitions.)

[6] Cf. *Deane papers*, I, 407.

[7] April 6, 1777, Colleville, pp. 133–35.

[8] Dekalb to Deane, December 18, 1776, *Deane papers*, I, 432.

[9] Dekalb to Broglie, September 24, 1777, A.A.E., Corr. Pol., E.-U., II, 235 v.

[10] "Inventaire des papiers de Louise-Auguste Montmorency, veuve de Charles Broglie," Archives Nationales, T 1608, no. 115. For possible evidence that La Colombe may also have been instigated by Broglie, see above, p. 108, and n. 15.

[11] See the petition of Delesser for promotion to the full rank of colonel (no date, but probably of 1779), in the S. W. Jackson Collection, Yale University Library.

Delesser also was the only one of the party who had been decorated with the Cross of St. Louis, though Dekalb reported a rumor to the effect that there were eighteen so decorated among them.[12]

Valfort eventually became the head of the École Militaire and one of those who taught Napoleon Bonaparte when he was a pupil at that school.[13] La Colombe became Lafayette's aide-de-camp in America and again during the French Revolution. Gimat and Brice also became his aides in the American Revolution.[14]

[12] Dekalb to Mme Dekalb, April 6, 1777, Colleville, p. 133.

[13] Cf. Ségur, I, 108. Ségur also mentions M. de Ternan as one of Lafayette's companions, but I find no trace of him upon the various lists of the "Victoire's" passengers.

[14] For what happened to the rest of the "caravan" see Kite, *loc. cit.*, pp. 148–78.

APPENDIX VII

San Sebastian or Los Pasajes; Marseilles or Toulon

Lafayette's *Mémoires* (I, 14 and 69) state that the "Victoire" made harbor at Los Pasajes in Spain after it left Bordeaux to avoid the expected orders from Paris. All of Lafayette's biographers have accepted this statement. Most contemporary sources, however, give San Sebastian as the port where they first anchored. The letters of Stormont (April 9), the Duc d'Ayen (April 11), Vergennes (April 11), Goltz (April 13), and Mme du Deffand (April 20), as well as the *Gazette de Leyde* (April 18) and the *Espion anglais* (May 26) (all cited in the pages above), state that the courier from Bordeaux found La-fayette at San Sebastian; none of them mentions Los Pasajes. That they were not wholly misinformed appears from letters of Dekalb. On March 26 he wrote from Verdon that they would "probably wait at St. Sebastian for the return of a courier sent to Paris."[1] On April 1 he dated a letter at San Sebas-tian,[2] stating that "we raised anchor the morning of the 26th with the inten-tion of anchoring here." Some question arises, nonetheless, whether the "Victoire" first sailed to the port of San Sebastian.

If it did, then when Lafayette left for Bordeaux and it appeared that he might be gone for several weeks, Dekalb must have decided that his vessel would be more hidden in the narrower and more secluded port of Los Pasajes. In that case he sailed her there sometime between April 1 and 6, for the letter of April 6 to Mme Dekalb is dated from Los Pasajes;[3] and on April 19, when he wrote to Deane, the place of writing is still indicated as Los Pasajes.[4] Stor-mont seems to have been informed of such change of moorings, as, in his letter to Weymouth of May 7, he says that Lafayette "is now known to have left St. Sebastian or a port in the neighborhood."[5] Lafayette's possible con-fusion can be seen as a result of his perturbation before he left San Sebastian and the excitement upon his return to Los Pasajes. Los Pasajes is closer to France than San Sebastian; San Sebastian is easier to enter or to leave. For

---

[1] Kapp, p. 104; confused by the difference between Lafayette's and Dekalb's testi-mony, Kapp says, "The Victoire first took a southerly course to Los Pasajes, a little port in the bay of St. Sebastian." This is a mistake. The ports of Los Pasajes and San Sebastian are separated from each other by several miles and a steep promontory.

[2] Colleville, p. 129.

[3] Kapp, p. 105; Colleville, p. 133.

[4] *Deane papers*, II, 47.

[5] P.R.O., S.P., France 78/302, no. 82.

that very reason the latter might be chosen for a vessel that wished to depart hurriedly and the former for one that wished to hide for several weeks. It seems most likely, however, that the "Victoire" sailed to Los Pasajes and remained there, though Lafayette and his companions visited San Sebastian.

A similar problem of geography arises with regard to the question whether the king's order required Lafayette to wait for the Duc d'Ayen and the Comtesse de Tessé at Marseilles or at Toulon. Dekalb's letters name both cities,[6] but the Duc d'Ayen's letter to Gérard says that Lafayette is "going to go to Marseilles in accordance with the king's orders."[7] The confusion arises easily from the fact that the party, after meeting at Marseilles, would have had to pass through Toulon in order to reach Italy.[8]

[6] Kapp, pp. 104–7; Colleville, p. 130.

[7] April 11, 1777, A.A.E., Corr. Pol., E.-U., II, 177.

[8] The original version of this appendix was found, after the first printing of this book, to have been partly mistaken: see Louis Gottschalk, *Lafayette joins the American army* (Chicago, 1937), p. 13. This appendix and the relevant passages elsewhere (see pp. 102, 113, and 121 above) have been revised accordingly.

APPENDIX VIII

Lafayette's Letter to Broglie

The copy of the alleged letter of the Marquis de Lafayette to the Comte de Broglie sent by Lord Stormont to Lord Weymouth on April 9, 1777,[1] reads (in translation) as follows:

BORDEAUX, March 23, 1777

I have the honor to inform you, Monsieur le Comte, that I am leaving for the country of which you know and upon that adventure which you advised me not to risk. You will be surprised at this step, but it would be impossible for me to act otherwise, and the proof of that fact is that I have not yielded to your advice. I have not even wanted to ask your opinion again because, with the best will in the world, Destiny would have prevented me, despite myself, from following it. You would have combatted my desires, I already had enough obstacles to surmount. Now there is so much less danger in confiding in you since my letter will leave for Paris at the very moment that I shall leave for Philadelphia, and it would then be futile to make me feel the inconvenience of a step already taken—to speak the common language, of a folly already committed. I even hope that you will be kind enough to help me and to encourage an enterprise that you no longer can prevent. For my part, I shall try to justify this frivolity (I admit the term) and to acquire the knowledge and the means whereby to distinguish myself.

This letter was either invented by the Comte de Broglie or was sent to him by prearrangement on his own solicitation. It is known only by means of this copy. Hence, we have as yet no way of knowing whether the text Broglie showed around was in Lafayette's handwriting or not. If the original should ever be found it will then be easy to determine whether it was Broglie's invention or was actually sent by Lafayette on Broglie's request.

The arguments against its complete authenticity are several. In the first place, the date alone is enough to render it suspicious. For in it Lafayette states "my letter will leave for Paris at the very moment that I shall leave for Philadelphia," and the "Victoire" did not leave until two days later. In fact, on March 23 Dekalb wrote his wife, "We are still ignorant whether our departure will not be prevented, as our vessel, so long detained already, cannot go out into the stream before tomorrow. When the wind will turn God only knows."[2] Yet, though dated March 23, Lafayette's letter might have been held over until March 25, when the wind changed, or even sent from Verdon on March 26; and the very sentence which raises our doubt might have been intended to convey that point.

There is, however, a later letter known to be authentic, written in La-

[1] P.R.O., S.P., France 78/302, no. 62.

[2] Kapp, p. 104.

fayette's hand, which completely contradicts the statements of the one in question. In this letter, written from America, on October 23, 1777, La-fayette seeks the elder Duboismartin's aid for another enterprise, a descent upon India. He says:

> I have not been able to refrain from submitting my plan to your judgment and that of M. le Comte de Broglie. If you do not find it unreasonable, will you please send my [inclosed] letter to the prime minister. . . . . A kind of *yes* from the minister would protect me from many inconveniences. . . . . Help me in my undertaking if it is under-takable. At least send the letter . . . . if it is sendable. You need not, I believe, appear to know its contents, and, as for M. le Comte de Broglie, he will judge whether it is worth while that he appear involved or whether it would be better that he know nothing too. I count so much upon his goodness, my confidence is so complete, that I do not doubt that he will interest himself in me in this affair as in the other.[3]

"The other" affair was, of course, the effort of Lafayette to go to America. This letter makes it perfectly plain that Lafayette knew Broglie's real atti-tude (even if not the motives thereof) toward his enterprise and renders dubious the pose of the earlier communication.

Suspicion of the authenticity of the Bordeaux letter is confirmed by the contents of the letter to Maurepas which Lafayette inclosed in the one just quoted. Lafayette here begged Maurepas for his co-operation in another "un-authorized" adventure somewhat like that which he had performed "without permission" in coming to America. A descent on India, he felt, could be easily accomplished "if I can hope from the government, not an order, not assistance, not, however, simple indifference, but a *je ne sais quoi*, for which no language furnishes me an expression delicate enough."[4] If Lafayette could in October, 1777, expect Duboismartin and Broglie to secure for him the prime minister's tacit approval to another "unauthorized" adventure, it could hardly have been because in March, 1777, he had been advised by that same Broglie not to undertake an earlier "unauthorized" one. Nor would he, some years later, have written in his *Mémoires* (I, 11) that Broglie had in the end helped him to go to America after at first exhibiting reluctance.

The easiest explanation of the Bordeaux message would be that it was a fiction invented by Broglie. One good argument for believing that Broglie wrote it himself is that he told Deane he had received it only on April 2 (at the moment when Deane was most anxious to be cleared of responsibility), though it was dated March 23; and (even if it had been sent off only on March 25 or 26, as considered above) it certainly did not take that long for the post to go from Bordeaux or Verdon to Paris. On the other hand, there is good ground for believing Lafayette actually wrote it, as prearranged with Dekalb, before they left Paris. In a letter that Deane wrote to the baron on March 22[5]

[3] Archives Nationales, AE^{II} 1018; facsimile in *Musée des Archives Nationales* (Paris, 1872), p. 617, where it is erroneously said to be addressed to the Comte de Broglie.

[4] Lafayette to Maurepas, October 24, 1777, A.A.E., Corr. Pol., E.-U., II, 250–51. This is published in Lafayette's *Mémoires*, I, 108–12, but erroneously said to be ad-dressed to Vergennes.

[5] *Deane papers*, II, 129.

there is an otherwise obscure sentence which bears directly upon this question: "You will remember the letters you mention from the Marquis, and favour me with one if you have time." If these were ordinary friendly letters or unsolicited reports of action from the marquis, why should Deane ask *Dekalb* to favor him with one from *Lafayette?* It would seem that Dekalb took upon himself the responsibility of inducing Lafayette to write Broglie and Deane letters that would shield them. Apparently Dekalb himself wrote similar letters.[6]

[6] See above, p. 110 and n. 21.

APPENDIX IX

Lafayette's Motives Described by Himself

In the Bibliothèque Nationale, N.A.F. 22738, folios 6–7, is the following letter (in French) addressed by Lafayette to Louis XVI, February 19, 1779. It is an effort to describe why he acted as he did when he disobeyed the king's order to accompany his relations into Italy. It must be remembered that by the time this letter was written Lafayette had spent almost two years in America and had begun to have quite decided notions of liberty and equality. But in endeavoring to make his peace with a Bourbon king, he avoided saying anything that might shock conservative sensibilities. The letter therefore reveals only what Lafayette as a French courtier thought in 1779.

SIRE

The unhappiness of having displeased Your Majesty produces so lively a sense of grief that it emboldens me, not to try to excuse a step that you disapprove, but to present the real motives which inspired it. My love for my country, my desire to witness the humiliation of her enemies, a political instinct which the last treaty [of 1778] would seem to justify—such are, Sire, the reasons which determined the part that I took in the American cause.

When I received Your Majesty's orders, I attributed them even more to the tender solicitude of my family than to a formula of conduct considered proper toward England. The emotions of my heart overcame my reason. I thought I could perceive that my departure would not be disapproved, just as surely as I saw the impossibility of permitting it; and if I added to my disobedience behavior which rendered me still more guilty, it is, Sire, because every Frenchman ought to risk his fortune, his hopes, and even public esteem rather than harm the interests of his country in compromising the government by his conduct.

Persuaded of my innocence, Sire, my heart was calm while fighting for my country. I enjoyed the pleasure of spilling my blood for her, and I permitted myself to offer homage to her with the slight services that I was able to render her allies. The first report of a war with England was about to send me back to France, when the arrival of Your Majesty's squadron and the opinion, always patriotic, always enlightened, of the General [d'Estaing] who commanded it persuaded me that my remaining in America would be more useful. . . . .

The chief significance of this letter for us is that it shows quite plainly that even as late as 1779 no one motive for his having gone to America had yet taken precedence in Lafayette's thought over the others and all were still so mixed in his mind that he could adapt them to the tastes of whatever group he had to address. For when it was written, France was an ally of the United States and expatiation upon the beauty of America's cause would have been less unwelcome than in 1777. A thoroughgoing enthusiast for the cause of liberty might easily have risked a philosophical phrase or two. A single-minded idealist might well have admitted his guilty sympathy for the cause of liberty, pointed out that it had brought distinct advantage to France, and begged to be excused or cheerfully faced the consequences. Such is the attitude the Lafayette of the next decade would have taken under like circumstances. Incidentally, too, the letter indicates that Lafayette, though he could hardly be expected to say to the king, "I did not think your orders were to be taken seriously," had thought of that possibility and was perfectly aware of two good reasons why they might not have been intended in earnest.

On several earlier occasions—at least when writing to Frenchmen—Lafayette made statements which, like those of his letter to the king, were meant to show that he had acted principally out of motives of French patriotism. On October 23, 1777, writing to Duboismartin, he described himself as "grievously tormented by the desire to prosecute something to the advantage of my vanity and the profit of my nation in this country"; and he went on to say: "In any case, do me the favor of telling me what you think about my coming back, about the good or bad effect it may produce. . . . . According to all appearances I shall remain here to fight the next campaign, if I receive no news. That of a declaration of war [by France on England] would decide me to leave immediately, even if I have to swim. . . . . If a descent on England is made, for God's sake, let me know about it."[1] Some months later (July 14, 1778) he made a like remark to the Comte d'Estaing:

If, while talking to you about public affairs, Monsieur le Comte, I were to take the time to speak to you of my own, I would tell you how embarrassing my situation is. Though agreeably situated in America, I have always thought, written and said everywhere here that I preferred to be a soldier under the French flag than a general anywhere else. It is my intention to leave immediately for the islands, Europe, even the Indies, if we are waging the war in any of these three parts of the world. . . . . If I did not have the hope that we [the Americans] will act in co-operation with the [French] fleet, I would board the first vessel and ask your permission to follow behind and as close to you as possible in order to be a witness of your success.[2]

To the members of his family Lafayette was also more emphatic regarding his French than his American patriotism. In a letter to the Duc d'Ayen of September 11, 1778, he wrote:

It is impossible to forecast when I shall have the happiness of being with you again. I shall act according to the circumstances. The big reason for my return would be a descent upon England. I would consider myself almost dishonored if I were not in it. I would be so ashamed and so displeased that I would want to drown myself or hang myself à l'anglaise. My greatest happiness would be to drive them out of here and then go into England.[3]

In the same mail he also wrote to Adrienne (September 13):

I used to think that the declaration of war [by France on England] would bring me to France immediately. Independent of all the bonds of affection which draw me toward the ones I love, my love for my country and my desire to serve her were among my motivating influences. I even feared that people who did not know me might suppose

---

[1] Archives Nationales, AE[II] 1018; see also above, p. 140.

[2] Henri Doniol, "Correspondance inédite de Lafayette," Revue d'histoire diplomatique, VI (1892), 404.

[3] Mémoires, I, 218.

that ambition for promotion, a love for the command that I have here, and the confidence with which I am honored would induce me to stay here some time longer. I declare that I would find a satisfaction in making these sacrifices for my country and to fly immediately to her aid without considering the one I would be leaving. . . . . [But M. d'Estaing] and the persons charged with the interests of France, like him, have told me that my departure would be contrary, and my remaining useful, to my country's service. I felt obliged to sacrifice my charming hopes, to postpone the realization of my most agreeable plans.[4]

It is quite clear from these declarations made to Frenchmen previous to 1780 that Lafayette acted in 1777—in large part at least—because of a desire to secure *revanche* for 1763; in other words, as a French aristocrat. The story that he sympathized with the American cause out of pure interest in democracy and the rights of man rests upon other statements made for American consumption or to Frenchmen after the American cult had become quite fashionable in France.

[4] *Ibid.*, pp. 221–22.

INDEX

(Names in italics indicate authors of bibliographical data.)